ENDYMION & THE LONGER POEMS OF JOHN KEATS

Cover: From *Diana and Endymion* by Francesco Trevisani

ISBN: 978-1-78139-260-7

Printed on acid-free ANSI archival quality paper.

© 2012 Benediction Classics, Oxford

ENDYMION

AND THE

LONGER POEMS

OF

JOHN KEATS

WITH NOTES BY

FRANCIS T. PALGRAVE

Contents

Endymion:
A Poetic Romance

"The stretched metre of an antique song"

PREFACE

(BY KEATS)

KNOWING within myself the manner in which this Poem has been produced, it is not without a feeling of regret that I make it public.

What manner I mean, will be quite clear to the reader, who must soon perceive great inexperience, immaturity, and every error denoting a feverish attempt, rather than a deed accomplished. The two first books, and indeed the two last, I feel sensible are not of such completion as to warrant their passing the press; nor should they if I thought a year's castigation would do them any good;—it will not: the foundations are too sandy. It is just that this youngster should die away: a sad thought for me, if I had not some hope that while it is dwindling I may be plotting, and fitting myself for verses fit to live.

This may be speaking too presumptuously, and may deserve a punishment: but no feeling man will be forward to inflict it: he will leave me alone, with the conviction that there is not a fiercer hell than the failure in a great object. This is not written with the least atom of purpose to forestall criticisms of course, but from the desire I have to conciliate men who are competent to look, and who do look with a zealous eye, to the honour of English literature.

The imagination of a boy is healthy, and the mature imagination of a man is healthy; but there is a space of life between, in which the soul is in a ferment, the character undecided, the way of life uncertain, the ambition thick-sighted: thence proceeds mawkishness, and all the thousand bitters which those men I speak of must necessarily taste in going over the following pages.

I hope I have not in too late a day touched the beautiful mythology of Greece, and dulled its brightness: for I wish to try once more, before I bid it farewel.

Teignmouth,
April 10, 1818.

INTRODUCTION

AS WITH other ancient legends, several variations of the story of Endymion have reached us. Keats has followed little except the mere outline of the simplest form: treating him as a Carian King, who slept on Mount Latmos, and was there visited by Selene. He has passed over the perpetual sleep which is the common point in the old stories, and, in itself, is sufficient to show that the modern interpretation, confidently making Endymion the Sun, and resolving the poetry of the myth into a mode of saying, "The sun sets behind a mountain, and the Moon rises over it," is as lame as it is prosaic.

Keats may have framed Peona, the name assigned to the sister with whom he provides Endymion, from *Pæana,* one of the minor heroines of the *Faerie Queene* (B. iv, C. 8 and 9): or he may have had in view Paean, the Healer or Deliverer;—the name given in Greek mythology to Asclepius.—But neither for this poem, nor for *Hyperion,* have I cared to enquire closely into names employed, or the allusions connected with them. They seem to be either derived from the common mythological works in use seventy years since, or invented by Keats himself. He has here a predecessor, perhaps a guide, in Spenser, who (with wider classical knowledge than Keats had reached), has handled classical legends in the same free, inventive way, and with the same indifference to correct scholarship.

Endymion, in truth, despite the name, is not, on the whole, more genuinely a Grecian tale than the *Faerie Queene.* Keats need not have feared, with his charming modesty, that he had here dulled the brightness of the beautiful mythology of Hellas. He has taken hardly more than that the goddess Selene loved the youth Endymion, from the old legend. It is not so much the canvas as the framework upon which he has woven and stretched a romantic piece of modern embroidery. To give this simple outline extension, a few of the best-known myths are introduced: they form the scenery, as it were, in and before which the long narrative of passion,—or, rather, the picture of passion, for *vera passio* is hardly here,—unfolds itself.—It is said that, on some one asking how Keats, the livery-stable-keeper's son, the surgeon's apprentice, could have learned his Grecian allusions, Shelley replied, "Because he *was* a Greek." In the enthusiastic warmth of this fine answer Shelley was, probably, thinking of *Hyperion,* the one poem which,—at any rate during the lifetime of Keats,—he admired. Even in that, however, we have really the same *romantic* (as opposed to *classical*) groundwork which we find in *Endymion,* presented under a Miltonic disguisal.

Where, then, are we to look for the Greek element in Keats? Chiefest and best I find it in that gift which only deserves the name because it is exhibited by Greek literature more perfectly and, on the whole, more continuously and consistently than by any other literature:—the gift of absolutely direct and, as it were, spontaneous expression of the thought, whether of description or of emotion, before the poet. Or rather, Nature herself appears to speak for him: the words come by inner law; they do not, as such, strike one either as prose or as poetry:—they seem as if they could not have been otherwise. This freedom from conventional colour or phrase, this Simplicity, in one word,—and Lucidity and Sanity with Simplicity,—is what marks all the great Hellenic poets, from Homer to the followers of Theocritus. When read closely, it is astonishing how little the diction differs from prose, whilst all the while it is felt to be the purest, the most essential, poetry. The early education of Keats had not given him the advantage of this experience, which, with longer life, he would doubtless have attained. Hence one may say that he has done his best, by overrichness of ornament, and by a vocabulary surcharged with Elizabethan verbal experiments and modern mannerism,—"luxury," to take a favourite word of his youth,—to conceal that native Hellenism which was recognized by Shelley. A similar criticism may be made, not unfrequently, upon the language of Shakespeare. And Shakespeare himself, also, has hardly displayed a nobler simplicity, a more complete and appropriate directness of speech, than Keats continually offers for our enjoyment. The freshness of phrase, going straight from his imagination to ours, the absolute sincerity and insight of the descriptive touches, even in the volume of 1817, are amazing. But these wonders, as Keats himself said upon Milton, "are, according to the great prerogative of poetry, better described in themselves than by a volume."—I had thought of adding examples; but the reader will enjoy them most, if left to his own chase after Beauty.

This word,—the one which arises first upon the mind, like sunshine, at the very name of Vergil, Mozart, or Flaxman,—is also our first, our truest, thought in the case of that child of genius, upon whom, with reverent diffidence, these notes are offered. Beauty, with him,— as with the Greeks above all the world,—is the first word and the last of Art; the one quality without which it is not. In this respect, again, Keats is a true son of Hellas. Yet, as he soon felt and acknowledged, in his early days it is too much the beautiful for beauty's sake only,—too much its outward visible form,—that he pursued. It is at this period that we find that splendid outburst of delight in pure natural loveliness which even he could hardly have bettered by verse:—"In truth, the great Elements we know of, are no mean comforters: the open sky sits upon our senses like a sapphire crown; the air is our robe of state; the earth is our throne, and the sea a mighty minstrel playing before it":— and again, "O for a life of sensations rather than of thoughts!"—It is not thus, however, that the greater poets of Greece thought and wrote. With them, (as indeed with most writers and artists till modern times), the landscape is persistently viewed in reference to human feeling and action, or, occasionally, to the presence of divine beings latent in or about stream and forest; rarely and cursorily painted for its own sake only. Nor, again, despite the Hellenic passion for simple, sensuous, beauty, (although pushed occasionally to a certain extravagance which has been sometimes taken for its normal expression), do the ancients announce such a worship of the Beautiful, in this external sense, for its own sake, as we find revealed in the earlier work of Keats. If they seem to say

Beauty is truth, truth beauty,

the Beautiful was taken in its wider and deeper meaning, carrying with it the ideas of eternal Law, of divine Justice, of the Theoretic happiness, man living on earth a life worthy of heaven, which the "Master of those who know" set forth as the final aim of human existence. In Beauty, thus considered,—Man, with his passions, his joys and griefs, his destiny,—the world beyond the world, the things beneath the veil,—formed necessarily the principal objects: and the *Lamia* and the *Eve of St. Agnes* show how soon our youthful poet began to move into that loftier sphere in which alone a thing of beauty can be a joy *for ever.*

For this first, simply-sensuous Beauty-worship, this picture of a world in which real humanity, with right and wrong, are not so much

6

excluded as not recognized, Keats might have found a precedent, not in "the beautiful mythology of Greece," referred to in the Preface to *Endymion,* but in the beginning of the later half of the Italian Renaissance; the great age of Florentine art and classicalism. It is, however, improbable that he could have drunk deeply, if at all, at that source: nor, as I shall presently endeavour to show, could he have derived his direction from his great Master, Spenser. He was, I conjecture, led in part by the tone of mind, bordering closely on a certain moral laxity, which he was conscious of in Leigh Hunt, mostly by the fervour and rush of perceptive and imaginative energy which boiled like a torrent through his youthful nature. I can best give an idea of this by a quotation,—which is not likely to be thought too long by any reader worthy of Keats,—from a letter written on his twenty-third birthday (29 Oct. 1818) to his dearly-loved brother George. Nowhere else, perhaps, is his innermost mind shown so freely: nor has any other Poet known to me made his confession with equal intensity and beauty of language, or given us such frank admission to the "mysteries of the studio."

"Notwithstanding your happiness and your recommendations, I hope I shall never marry: though the most beautiful creature were waiting for me at the end of a journey or a walk; though the carpet were of silk, and the curtains of the morning clouds, the chairs and sofas stuffed with cygnet's down, the food manna, the wine beyond claret, the window opening on Winandermere, I should not feel, or rather my happiness should not be, so fine; my solitude is sublime— for, instead of what I have described, there is a sublimity to welcome me home; the roaring of the wind is my wife; and the stars through the window-panes are my children; the mighty abstract Idea of Beauty in all things, I have, stifles the more divided and minute domestic happiness.... I feel more and more every day, as my imagination strengthens, that I do not live in this world alone, but in a thousand worlds. No sooner am I alone, than shapes of epic greatness are stationed around me, and serve my spirit the office which is equivalent to a King's Body-guard: "then Tragedy with scepter'd pall comes sweeping by:" according to my state of mind, I am with Achilles shouting in the trenches, or with Theocritus in the vales of Sicily; or throw my whole being into Troilus, and, repeating those lines, "I wander like a lost soul upon the Stygian bank, staying for waftage," I melt into the air with a voluptuousness so delicate, that I am content to be alone."

The letters of Keats, and, in some degree, his last poems, show that it was not from want of manly power, lofty purpose, or interest in humanity, that he thought and wrote in this almost Epicurean strain:— although it is idle to conjecture in what direction his great genius,— greater in promise, as his illustrious successor in Poetry has more than once remarked to me, than any born among us since Milton,—would have exhibited its maturity. The want of high, human, aim in its noblest sense is, however, the point in which Keats most differs from that Master to whom in early youth he was mainly indebted. In the prefatory letter to the *Faerie Queene* Spenser,—"our sage and serious Spenser," as Milton named him,—himself sets forth as his object, "to fashion a gentleman or a noble person in vertuous and gentle discipline." "No one," says Mr. Aubrey de Vere in a recent Essay, published in Dr. Grosart's edition, "no one was more familiar with forest scenery, or with the charm of mead and meadow and river-bank; but he left it for poets of a later age to find in natural description the chief sphere for the exercise of their faculties. He lived too near the chivalrous age of action and passion.... His imagination and his affections followed the mediæval type. All that he saw was to him the emblem of things unseen; the material world thus became the sacrament of a spiritual world, and the earthly life a betrothal to a life beyond the grave." So Professor Dowden, in his equally able Essay:— "The high distinction of Spenser's poetry is to be found in the rare degree in which it unites sense and soul, moral seriousness and the Renaissance appetite for beauty.... With all its opulence of colour and melody, with all its imagery of delight, the "Faerie Queene" has primarily a moral or spiritual intention. While Spenser sees the abundant beauty of the world, and the splendour of man and of the life of man, his vision of human life is grave and even stern."

It will easily be seen how far the *Endymion* falls below this ideal, and suffers, hence, in sustained interest. In one element, indeed, he was without Spenser's advantage:—Mediaeval types, as employed throughout the *Faerie Queene* were not available for Keats. That element he has replaced by recurrence to Grecian mythology. And,— had he rendered this in its vital essence, though more remote in time than Mediaevalism, its beauty and its breadth of human nature might have supplied some compensation. As it is, the somewhat external Hellenism which he reproduced here and (though in severer style) in *Hyperion,* was incapable of supplying adequate body or unity to the narrative. These poems want the unifying "architectonic" faculty:—the

8

"touch of nature" that gives life to the whole.—But the Poet, (whose perfect modesty in regard to his own work is in curious contrast with the over-frequent self-laudation of Spenser), himself remarked upon *Endymion:* "I have most likely but moved into the go-cart from the leading-strings."

As a true artist, Keats knew his own deficiencies: nor does Shelley's estimate of *Endymion,* both at the time of publication and when he wrote his letter of remonstrance to Mr. Gifford, (1820), view the poem more favourably. It would be more agreeable to dwell here upon the magical beauties of detail which even in Spenser himself are not more frequent or more magical. One might transfer Ben Jonson's name for his own minor poems to *Endymion:* It is not so much a forest, as *Underwoods.* Or we may think of the *luxuria foliorum* of that tree in the Garden of Proserpine described by Spenser,

Clothed with leaves, that none the wood mote see,
And loaden all with fruit as thick as it might bee.

Splendid as are the foliage and the flowers, *Endymion* is an almost pathless intricacy of story: a Paradise without a plan. What page, however, is there here in which the Poet does not give us lines or touches so fresh, so vigorous, so directly going to the very heart of Nature, that more of essential Poetry is concentrated in one than can be found in whole volumes by his imitators? I had marked many such phrases:—but, as noticed before, they are best left for the reader's delight and discernment. Meanwhile, a few words by the Poet's biographer may close this over-lengthy attempt. "Let us never forget," says Lord Houghton, "that, wonderful as are the poems of Keats, yet, after all, they are rather the records of a poetical education, than the accomplished work of the mature artist." Even thus, however, what poet, in the whole range of literature, at twenty-four, has rivalled them?

Endymion

BOOK I

A THING of beauty is a joy for ever:
Its loveliness increases; it will never
Pass into nothingness; but still will keep
A bower quiet for us, and a sleep
Full of sweet dreams, and health, and quiet breathing.   5
Therefore, on every morrow, are we wreathing
A flowery band to bind us to the earth,
Spite of despondence, of the inhuman dearth
Of noble natures, of the gloomy days,
Of all the unhealthy and o'er-darkened ways   10
Made for our searching: yes, in spite of all,
Some shape of beauty moves away the pall
From our dark spirits. Such the sun, the moon,
Trees old and young, sprouting a shady boon
For simple sheep; and such are daffodils   15
With the green world they live in; and clear rills
That for themselves a cooling covert make
'Gainst the hot season; the mid forest brake,
Rich with a sprinkling of fair musk-rose blooms:
And such too is the grandeur of the dooms   20
We have imagined for the mighty dead;
All lovely tales that we have heard or read:
An endless fountain of immortal drink,
Pouring unto us from the heaven's brink.

Nor do we merely feel these essences   25
For one short hour; no, even as the trees
That whisper round a temple become soon

Dear as the temple's self, so does the moon,
The passion poesy, glories infinite,
Haunt us till they become a cheering light   30
Unto our souls, and bound to us so fast,
That, whether there be shine, or gloom o'ercast,
They alway must be with us, or we die.

Therefore, 'tis with full happiness that I
Will trace the story of Endymion.   35
The very music of the name has gone
Into my being, and each pleasant scene
Is growing fresh before me as the green
Of our own vallies: so I will begin[1]
Now while I cannot hear the city's din;   40
Now while the early budders are just new,
And run in mazes of the youngest hue
About old forests; while the willow trails
Its delicate amber; and the dairy pails
Bring home increase of milk. And, as the year   45
Grows lush in juicy stalks, I'll smoothly steer
My little boat, for many quiet hours,
With streams that deepen freshly into bowers.
Many and many a verse I hope to write,
Before the daisies, vermeil rimm'd and white,   50
Hide in deep herbage; and ere yet the bees
Hum about globes of clover and sweet peas,
I must be near the middle of my story.
O may no wintry season, bare and hoary,

---

[1] l. 39–57 *Endymion* was begun, (it seems at Carisbrooke), April 1817: by September following, (at Oxford), he had reached B. iii: B. iv was finished on 28 November: B. i was given to the publisher January 1818. "I am anxious to get *Endymion* printed that I may forget it, and proceed," Keats says with his usual utter and delightful modesty, in a letter of 27 February. The lovely Preface is dated 10 April.

See it half finished: but let Autumn bold,   55
With universal tinge of sober gold,
Be all about me when I make an end.
And now at once, adventuresome, I send
My herald thought into a wilderness:
There let its trumpet blow, and quickly dress   60
My uncertain path with green, that I may speed
Easily onward, thorough flowers and weed.

   Upon the sides of Latmos was outspread
A mighty forest; for the moist earth fed
So plenteously all weed-hidden roots   65
Into o'er-hanging boughs, and precious fruits.
And it had gloomy shades, sequestered deep,
Where no man went; and if from shepherd's keep
A lamb strayed far a-down those inmost glens,
Never again saw he the happy pens   70
Whither his brethren, bleating with content,
Over the hills at every nightfall went.
Among the shepherds, 'twas believed ever,
That not one fleecy lamb which thus did sever
From the white flock, but pass'd unworried   75
By angry wolf, or pard with prying head,
Until it came to some unfooted plains
Where fed the herds of Pan: ay great his gains
Who thus one lamb did lose. Paths there were many,
Winding through palmy fern, and rushes fenny,   80
And ivy banks; all leading pleasantly
To a wide lawn, whence one could only see
Stems thronging all around between the swell
Of turf and slanting branches: who could tell
The freshness of the space of heaven above,   85
Edg'd round with dark tree tops? through which a dove

Would often beat its wings, and often too
A little cloud would move across the blue.

  Full in the middle of this pleasantness
There stood a marble altar, with a tress   90
Of flowers budded newly; and the dew
Had taken fairy phantasies to strew
Daisies upon the sacred sward last eve,
And so the dawned light in pomp receive.
For 'twas the morn: Apollo's upward fire   95
Made every eastern cloud a silvery pyre
Of brightness so unsullied, that therein
A melancholy spirit well might win
Oblivion, and melt out his essence fine
Into the winds: rain-scented eglantine   100
Gave temperate sweets to that well-wooing sun;
The lark was lost in him; cold springs had run
To warm their chilliest bubbles in the grass;
Man's voice was on the mountains; and the mass
Of nature's lives and wonders puls'd tenfold,   105
To feel this sun-rise and its glories old.

  Now while the silent workings of the dawn
Were busiest, into that self-same lawn
All suddenly, with joyful cries, there sped
A troop of little children garlanded;   110
Who gathering round the altar, seemed to pry
Earnestly round as wishing to espy
Some folk of holiday: nor had they waited
For many moments, ere their ears were sated
With a faint breath of music, which ev'n then   115
Fill'd out its voice, and died away again.
Within a little space again it gave
Its airy swellings, with a gentle wave,

To light-hung leaves, in smoothest echoes breaking
Through copse-clad vallies,—ere their death, oer-taking 120
The surgy murmurs of the lonely sea.

And now, as deep into the wood as we
Might mark a lynx's eye, there glimmered light
Fair faces and a rush of garments white,
Plainer and plainer shewing, till at last   125
Into the widest alley they all past,
Making directly for the woodland altar.
O kindly muse! let not my weak tongue faulter
In telling of this goodly company,
Of their old piety, and of their glee: 130
But let a portion of ethereal dew
Fall on my head, and presently unmew
My soul; that I may dare, in wayfaring,
To stammer where old Chaucer used to sing.

Leading the way, young damsels danced along,   135
Bearing the burden of a shepherd song;
Each having a white wicker over brimm'd
With April's tender younglings: next, well trimm'd,
A crowd of shepherds with as sunburnt looks
As may be read of in Arcadian books;   140
Such as sat listening round Apollo's pipe,
When the great deity, for earth too ripe,
Let his divinity o'er-flowing die
In music, through the vales of Thessaly:
Some idly trailed their sheep-hooks on the ground,   145
And some kept up a shrilly mellow sound
With ebon-tipped flutes: close after these,
Now coming from beneath the forest trees,
A venerable priest full soberly,
Begirt with ministring looks: alway his eye   150

Stedfast upon the matted turf he kept,
And after him his sacred vestments swept.
From his right hand there swung a vase, milk-white,
Of mingled wine, out-sparkling generous light;
And in his left he held a basket full   155
Of all sweet herbs that searching eye could cull:
Wild thyme, and valley-lilies whiter still
Than Leda's love, and cresses from the rill.
His aged head, crowned with beechen wreath,
Seem'd like a poll of ivy in the teeth   160
Of winter hoar. Then came another crowd
Of shepherds, lifting in due time aloud
Their share of the ditty. After them appear'd,
Up-followed by a multitude that rear'd
Their voices to the clouds, a fair wrought car,   165
Easily rolling so as scarce to mar
The freedom of three steeds of dapple brown:
Who stood therein did seem of great renown
Among the throng. His youth was fully blown,
Shewing like Ganymede to manhood grown;   170
And, for those simple times, his garments were
A chieftain king's: beneath his breast, half bare,
Was hung a silver bugle, and between
His nervy knees there lay a boar-spear keen.
A smile was on his countenance; he seem'd,   175
To common lookers on, like one who dream'd
Of idleness in groves Elysian:
But there were some who feelingly could scan
A lurking trouble in his nether lip,
And see that oftentimes the reins would slip   180
Through his forgotten hands: then would they sigh,
And think of yellow leaves, of owlets cry,
Of logs piled solemnly.—Ah, well-a-day,
Why should our young Endymion pine away!

Soon the assembly, in a circle rang'd,   185
Stood silent round the shrine: each look was chang'd
To sudden veneration: women meek
Beckon'd their sons to silence; while each cheek
Of virgin bloom paled gently for slight fear.
Endymion too, without a forest peer,   190
Stood, wan, and pale, and with an awed face,
Among his brothers of the mountain chase.
In midst of all, the venerable priest
Eyed them with joy from greatest to the least,
And, after lifting up his aged hands,   195
Thus spake he: "Men of Latmos! shepherd bands!
Whose care it is to guard a thousand flocks:
Whether descended from beneath the rocks
That overtop your mountains; whether come
From vallies where the pipe is never dumb;   200
Or from your swelling downs, where sweet air stirs
Blue hare-bells lightly, and where prickly furze
Buds lavish gold; or ye, whose precious charge
Nibble their fill at ocean's very marge,
Whose mellow reeds are touch'd with sounds forlorn 205
By the dim echoes of old Triton's horn:
Mothers and wives! who day by day prepare
The scrip, with needments, for the mountain air;
And all ye gentle girls who foster up
Udderless lambs, and in a little cup   210
Will put choice honey for a favoured youth:
Yea, every one attend! for in good truth
Our vows are wanting to our great god Pan.
Are not our lowing heifers sleeker than
Night-swollen mushrooms? Are not our wide plains 215
Speckled with countless fleeces? Have not rains
Green'd over April's lap? No howling sad
Sickens our fearful ewes; and we have had

Great bounty from Endymion our lord.
The earth is glad: the merry lark has pour'd   220
His early song against yon breezy sky,
That spreads so clear o'er our solemnity."

Thus ending, on the shrine he heap'd a spire
Of teeming sweets, enkindling sacred fire;
Anon he stain'd the thick and spongy sod   225
With wine, in honour of the shepherd-god.
Now while the earth was drinking it, and while
Bay leaves were crackling in the fragrant pile,
And gummy frankincense was sparkling bright
'Neath smothering parsley, and a hazy light   230
Spread greyly eastward, thus a chorus sang:

"O THOU, whose mighty palace roof doth hang
From jagged trunks, and overshadoweth
Eternal whispers, glooms, the birth, life, death
Of unseen flowers in heavy peacefulness;   235
Who lov'st to see the hamadryads dress
Their ruffled locks where meeting hazels darken;
And through whole solemn hours dost sit, and hearken
The dreary melody of bedded reeds—
In desolate places, where dank moisture breeds   240
The pipy hemlock to strange overgrowth;
Bethinking thee, how melancholy loth
Thou wast to lose fair Syrinx—do thou now,
By thy love's milky brow!
By all the trembling mazes that she ran,   245
Hear us, great Pan!

"O thou, for whose soul-soothing quiet, turtles
Passion their voices cooingly 'mong myrtles,
What time thou wanderest at eventide

Through sunny meadows, that outskirt the side 250
Of thine enmossed realms: O thou, to whom
Broad leaved fig trees even now foredoom
Their ripen'd fruitage; yellow girted bees
Their golden honeycombs; our village leas
Their fairest-blossom'd beans and poppied corn; 255
The chuckling linnet its five young unborn,
To sing for thee; low creeping strawberries
Their summer coolness; pent up butterflies
Their freckled wings; yea, the fresh budding year
All its completions—be quickly near, 260
By every wind that nods the mountain pine,
O forester divine!

    "Thou, to whom every fawn and satyr flies
For willing service; whether to surprise
The squatted hare while in half sleeping fit; 265
Or upward ragged precipices flit
To save poor lambkins from the eagle's maw;
Or by mysterious enticement draw
Bewildered shepherds to their path again;
Or to tread breathless round the frothy main, 270
And gather up all fancifullest shells
For thee to tumble into Naiads' cells,
And, being hidden, laugh at their out-peeping;
Or to delight thee with fantastic leaping,
The while they pelt each other on the crown 275
With silvery oak apples, and fir cones brown—
By all the echoes that about thee ring,
Hear us, O satyr king!

    "O Hearkener to the loud clapping shears,
While ever and anon to his shorn peers 280
A ram goes bleating: Winder of the horn,

19

When snouted wild-boars routing tender corn
Anger our huntsman: Breather round our farms,
To keep off mildews, and all weather harms:
Strange ministrant of undescribed sounds,   285
That come a swooning over hollow grounds,
And wither drearily on barren moors:
Dread opener of the mysterious doors
Leading to universal knowledge—see,
Great son of Dryope,   290
The many that are come to pay their vows
With leaves about their brows!

   Be still the unimaginable lodge
For solitary thinkings; such as dodge
Conception to the very bourne of heaven,   295
Then leave the naked brain: be still the leaven,
That spreading in this dull and clodded earth
Gives it a touch ethereal—a new birth:
Be still a symbol of immensity;
A firmament reflected in a sea;   300
An element filling the space between;
An unknown—but no more: we humbly screen
With uplift hands our foreheads, lowly bending,
And giving out a shout most heaven rending,
Conjure thee to receive our humble Paean,   305
Upon thy Mount Lycean!

   Even while they brought the burden to a close,
A shout from the whole multitude arose,
That lingered in the air like dying rolls
Of abrupt thunder, when Ionian shoals   310
Of dolphins bob their noses through the brine.
Meantime, on shady levels, mossy fine,
Young companies nimbly began dancing

To the swift treble pipe, and humming string.
Aye, those fair living forms swam heavenly   315
To tunes forgotten—out of memory:
Fair creatures! whose young children's children bred
Thermopylæ its heroes—not yet dead,
But in old marbles ever beautiful.
High genitors, unconscious did they cull   320
Time's sweet first-fruits—they danc'd to weariness,
And then in quiet circles did they press
The hillock turf, and caught the latter end
Of some strange history, potent to send
A young mind from its bodily tenement.   325
Or they might watch the quoit-pitchers, intent
On either side; pitying the sad death
Of Hyacinthus, when the cruel breath
Of Zephyr slew him,—Zephyr penitent,
Who now, ere Phoebus mounts the firmament,   330
Fondles the flower amid the sobbing rain.
The archers too, upon a wider plain,
Beside the feathery whizzing of the shaft,
And the dull twanging bowstring, and the raft[2]
Branch down sweeping from a tall ash top,   335
Call'd up a thousand thoughts to envelope
Those who would watch. Perhaps, the trembling knee
And frantic gape of lonely Niobe,
Poor, lonely Niobe! when her lovely young
Were dead and gone, and her caressing tongue   340
Lay a lost thing upon her paly lip,
And very, very deadliness did nip
Her motherly cheeks. Arous'd from this sad mood

---

[2] l. 334 *the raft Branch*: Apparently, the branch torn off. Keats, who may have taken the word from Spenser, appears either not to have noticed the want of a syllable in l. 335, or to have satisfied his ear with the words as they stand.

By one, who at a distance loud halloo'd,
Uplifting his strong bow into the air,   345
Many might after brighter visions stare:
After the Argonauts, in blind amaze
Tossing about on Neptune's restless ways,
Until, from the horizon's vaulted side,
There shot a golden splendour far and wide,   350
Spangling those million poutings of the brine
With quivering ore: 'twas even an awful shine
From the exaltation of Apollo's bow;
A heavenly beacon in their dreary woe.
Who thus were ripe for high contemplating,   355
Might turn their steps towards the sober ring
Where sat Endymion and the aged priest
'Mong shepherds gone in eld, whose looks increas'd
The silvery setting of their mortal star.
There they discours'd upon the fragile bar   360
That keeps us from our homes ethereal;
And what our duties there: to nightly call
Vesper, the beauty-crest of summer weather;
To summon all the downiest clouds together
For the sun's purple couch; to emulate   365
In ministring the potent rule of fate
With speed of fire-tailed exhalations;
To tint her pallid cheek with bloom, who cons
Sweet poesy by moonlight: besides these,
A world of other unguess'd offices.   370
Anon they wander'd, by divine converse,
Into Elysium; vieing to rehearse
Each one his own anticipated bliss.
One felt heart-certain that he could not miss
His quick gone love, among fair blossom'd boughs,   375
Where every zephyr-sigh pouts and endows
Her lips with music for the welcoming.

Another wish'd, mid that eternal spring,
To meet his rosy child, with feathery sails,
Sweeping, eye-earnestly, through almond vales: 380
Who, suddenly, should stoop through the smooth wind,
And with the balmiest leaves his temples bind;
And, ever after, through those regions be
His messenger, his little Mercury.
Some were athirst in soul to see again   385
Their fellow huntsmen o'er the wide champaign
In times long past; to sit with them, and talk
Of all the chances in their earthly walk;
Comparing, joyfully, their plenteous stores
Of happiness, to when upon the moors,   390
Benighted, close they huddled from the cold,
And shar'd their famish'd scrips. Thus all out-told
Their fond imaginations,—saving him
Whose eyelids curtain'd up their jewels dim,
Endymion: yet hourly had he striven   395
To hide the cankering venom, that had riven
His fainting recollections. Now indeed
His senses had swoon'd off: he did not heed
The sudden silence, or the whispers low,
Or the old eyes dissolving at his woe,   400
Or anxious calls, or close of trembling palms,
Or maiden's sigh, that grief itself embalms:
But in the self-same fixed trance he kept,
Like one who on the earth had never stept.
Aye, even as dead-still as a marble man,   405
Frozen in that old tale Arabian.

    Who whispers him so pantingly and close?
Peona, his sweet sister: of all those,
His friends, the dearest. Hushing signs she made,
And breath'd a sister's sorrow to persuade   410

23

A yielding up, a cradling on her care.[3]
Her eloquence did breathe away the curse:
She led him, like some midnight spirit nurse
Of happy changes in emphatic dreams,
Along a path between two little streams,—   415
Guarding his forehead, with her round elbow,
From low-grown branches, and his footsteps slow
From stumbling over stumps and hillocks small;
Until they came to where these streamlets fall,
With mingled bubblings and a gentle rush,   420
Into a river, clear, brimful, and flush
With crystal mocking of the trees and sky.
A little shallop, floating there hard by,
Pointed its beak over the fringed bank;
And soon it lightly dipt, and rose, and sank,   425
And dipt again, with the young couple's weight,—
Peona guiding, through the water straight,
Towards a bowery island opposite;
Which gaining presently, she steered light
Into a shady, fresh, and ripply cove,   430
Where nested was an arbour, overwove
By many a summer's silent fingering;
To whose cool bosom she was used to bring
Her playmates, with their needle broidery,
And minstrel memories of times gone by.   435

     So she was gently glad to see him laid
Under her favourite bower's quiet shade,
On her own couch, new made of flower leaves,
Dried carefully on the cooler side of sheaves
When last the sun his autumn tresses shook,   440

---

[3] l. 411   The last word of this line, with eight others in *Endymion*, is,—I do not doubt, intentionally,—left without a rhyme.

And the tann'd harvesters rich armfuls took.
Soon was he quieted to slumbrous rest:
But, ere it crept upon him, he had prest
Peona's busy hand against his lips,
And still, a sleeping, held her finger-tips   445
In tender pressure. And as a willow keeps
A patient watch over the stream that creeps
Windingly by it, so the quiet maid
Held her in peace: so that a whispering blade
Of grass, a wailful gnat, a bee bustling   450
Down in the blue-bells, or a wren light rustling
Among seer leaves and twigs, might all be heard.

O magic sleep! O comfortable bird,
That broodest o'er the troubled sea of the mind
Till it is hush'd and smooth! O unconfin'd   455
Restraint! imprisoned liberty! great key
To golden palaces, strange minstrelsy,
Fountains grotesque, new trees, bespangled caves,
Echoing grottos, full of tumbling waves
And moonlight; aye, to all the mazy world   460
Of silvery enchantment!—who, upfurl'd
Beneath thy drowsy wing a triple hour,
But renovates and lives?—Thus, in the bower,
Endymion was calm'd to life again.
Opening his eyelids with a healthier brain,   465
He said: "I feel this thine endearing love
All through my bosom: thou art as a dove
Trembling its closed eyes and sleeked wings
About me; and the pearliest dew not brings
Such morning incense from the fields of May,   470
As do those brighter drops that twinkling stray

From those kind eyes,[4]—the very home and haunt
Of sisterly affection. Can I want
Aught else, aught nearer heaven, than such tears?
Yet dry them up, in bidding hence all fears   475
That, any longer, I will pass my days
Alone and sad. No, I will once more raise
My voice upon the mountain-heights; once more
Make my horn parley from their foreheads hoar:
Again my trooping hounds their tongues shall loll   480
Around the breathed boar: again I'll poll
The fair-grown yew tree, for a chosen bow:
And, when the pleasant sun is getting low,
Again I'll linger in a sloping mead
To hear the speckled thrushes, and see feed   485
Our idle sheep. So be thou cheered sweet,
And, if thy lute is here, softly intreat
My soul to keep in its resolved course."

　　Hereat Peona, in their silver source,
Shut her pure sorrow drops with glad exclaim,   490
And took a lute, from which there pulsing came
A lively prelude, fashioning the way
In which her voice should wander. 'Twas a lay
More subtle cadenced, more forest wild[5]
Than Dryope's lone lulling of her child;   495
And nothing since has floated in the air
So mournful strange. Surely some influence rare

---

[4] l. 472–3 One of the rare touches of exquisite human feeling which Keats has allowed himself,—perhaps, which his chosen subject and treatment allowed him,—in *Endymion:*—a poem, under this aspect, curiously contrasted with the *Isabella* and the *St. Agnes.*

[5] l. 493–5 "A substantive," says Professor Earle, "may suddenly by a vigorous stroke of art be transformed into an adverb, as *forest* in the following passage:
　　　　　more forest wild."
(*Philology of the English Tongue:* 1873).

Went, spiritual, through the damsel's hand;
For still, with Delphic emphasis, she spann'd
The quick invisible strings, even though she saw   500
Endymion's spirit melt away and thaw
Before the deep intoxication.
But soon she came, with sudden burst, upon
Her self-possession—swung the lute aside,
And earnestly said: "Brother, 'tis vain to hide   505
That thou dost know of things mysterious,
Immortal, starry; such alone could thus
Weigh down thy nature. Hast thou sinn'd in aught
Offensive to the heavenly powers? Caught
A Paphian dove upon a message sent?   510
Thy deathful bow against some deer-herd bent,
Sacred to Dian? Haply, thou hast seen
Her naked limbs among the alders green;
And that, alas! is death. No, I can trace
Something more high perplexing in thy face!"   515

    Endymion look'd at her, and press'd her hand,
And said, "Art thou so pale, who wast so bland
And merry in our meadows? How is this?
Tell me thine ailment: tell me all amiss!—
Ah! thou hast been unhappy at the change   520
Wrought suddenly in me. What indeed more strange?
Or more complete to overwhelm surmise?
Ambition is no sluggard: 'tis no prize,
That toiling years would put within my grasp,
That I have sigh'd for: with so deadly gasp   525
No man e'er panted for a mortal love.
So all have set my heavier grief above
These things which happen. Rightly have they done:
I, who still saw the horizontal sun
Heave his broad shoulder o'er the edge of the world,   530

27

Out-facing Lucifer, and then had hurl'd
My spear aloft, as signal for the chace—
I, who, for very sport of heart, would race
With my own steed from Araby; pluck down
A vulture from his towery perching; frown   535
A lion into growling, loth retire—
To lose, at once, all my toil breeding fire,
And sink thus low! but I will ease my breast
Of secret grief, here in this bowery nest.

"This river does not see the naked sky,   540
Till it begins to progress silverly
Around the western border of the wood,
Whence, from a certain spot, its winding flood
Seems at the distance like a crescent moon:
And in that nook, the very pride of June,   545
Had I been used to pass my weary eves;
The rather for the sun unwilling leaves
So dear a picture of his sovereign power,
And I could witness his most kingly hour,
When he doth lighten up the golden reins,   550
And paces leisurely down amber plains
His snorting four. Now when his chariot last
Its beams against the zodiac-lion cast,
There blossom'd suddenly a magic bed
Of sacred ditamy,[6] and poppies red: 555
At which I wondered greatly, knowing well
That but one night had wrought this flowery spell;
And, sitting down close by, began to muse
What it might mean. Perhaps, thought I, Morpheus,
In passing here, his owlet pinions shook;   560

---

[6] l. 555 *ditamy,* dittany: In Old French, *dictame*; whence, probably, the spelling used by Keats.

Or, it may be, ere matron Night uptook
Her ebon urn, young Mercury, by stealth,
Had dipt his rod in it: such garland wealth
Came not by common growth. Thus on I thought,
Until my head was dizzy and distraught.   565
Moreover, through the dancing poppies stole
A breeze, most softly lulling to my soul;
And shaping visions all about my sight
Of colours, wings, and bursts of spangly light;
The which became more strange, and strange, and dim,   570
And then were gulph'd in a tumultuous swim:
And then I fell asleep. Ah, can I tell
The enchantment that afterwards befel?
Yet it was but a dream: yet such a dream
That never tongue, although it overteem   575
With mellow utterance, like a cavern spring,
Could figure out and to conception bring
All I beheld and felt. Methought I lay
Watching the zenith, where the milky way
Among the stars in virgin splendour pours;   580
And travelling my eye, until the doors
Of heaven appear'd to open for my flight,
I became loth and fearful to alight
From such high soaring by a downward glance:
So kept me stedfast in that airy trance,   585
Spreading imaginary pinions wide.
When, presently, the stars began to glide,
And faint away, before my eager view:
At which I sigh'd that I could not pursue,
And dropt my vision to the horizon's verge;   590
And lo! from opening clouds, I saw emerge
The loveliest moon, that ever silver'd o'er
A shell for Neptune's goblet: she did soar
So passionately bright, my dazzled soul

Commingling with her argent spheres did roll   595
Through clear and cloudy, even when she went
At last into a dark and vapoury tent—
Whereat, methought, the lidless-eyed train
Of planets all were in the blue again.
To commune with those orbs, once more I rais'd   600
My sight right upward: but it was quite dazed
By a bright something, sailing down apace,
Making me quickly veil my eyes and face:
Again I look'd, and, O ye deities,
Who from Olympus watch our destinies!   605
Whence that completed form of all completeness?
Whence came that high perfection of all sweetness?
Speak, stubborn earth, and tell me where, O Where
Hast thou a symbol of her golden hair?
Not oat-sheaves drooping in the western sun;   610
Not—thy soft hand, fair sister! let me shun
Such follying before thee—yet she had,
Indeed, locks bright enough to make me mad;
And they were simply gordian'd up and braided,
Leaving, in naked comeliness, unshaded,   615
Her pearl round ears, white neck, and orbed brow;
The which were blended in, I know not how,
With such a paradise of lips and eyes,
Blush-tinted cheeks, half smiles, and faintest sighs,
That, when I think thereon, my spirit clings   620
And plays about its fancy, till the stings
Of human neighbourhood envenom all.
Unto what awful power shall I call?
To what high fane?—Ah! see her hovering feet,
More bluely vein'd, more soft, more whitely sweet   625
Than those of sea-born Venus, when she rose
From out her cradle shell. The wind out-blows
Her scarf into a fluttering pavilion;

'Tis blue, and over-spangled with a million
Of little eyes, as though thou wert to shed,   630
Over the darkest, lushest blue-bell bed,
Handfuls of daisies."—"Endymion, how strange!
Dream within dream!"—"She took an airy range,
And then, towards me, like a very maid,
Came blushing, waning, willing, and afraid,   635
And press'd me by the hand: Ah! 'twas too much;
Methought I fainted at the charmed touch,
Yet held my recollection, even as one
Who dives three fathoms where the waters run
Gurgling in beds of coral: for anon,   640
I felt upmounted in that region
Where falling stars dart their artillery forth,
And eagles struggle with the buffeting north
That balances the heavy meteor-stone;—
Felt too, I was not fearful, nor alone,   645
But lapp'd and lull'd along the dangerous sky.
Soon, as it seem'd, we left our journeying high,
And straightway into frightful eddies swoop'd;
Such as ay muster where grey time has scoop'd
Huge dens and caverns in a mountain's side: 650
There hollow sounds arous'd me, and I sigh'd
To faint once more by looking on my bliss—
I was distracted; madly did I kiss
The wooing arms which held me, and did give
My eyes at once to death: but 'twas to live,   655
To take in draughts of life from the gold fount
Of kind and passionate looks; to count, and count
The moments, by some greedy help that seem'd
A second self, that each might be redeem'd
And plunder'd of its load of blessedness.   660
Ah, desperate mortal! I ev'n dar'd to press
Her very cheek against my crowned lip,

And, at that moment, felt my body dip
Into a warmer air: a moment more,
Our feet were soft in flowers. There was store   665
Of newest joys upon that alp. Sometimes
A scent of violets, and blossoming limes,
Loiter'd around us; then of honey cells,
Made delicate from all white-flower bells;
And once, above the edges of our nest,   670
An arch face peep'd,—an Oread as I guess'd.

    "Why did I dream that sleep o'er-power'd me
In midst of all this heaven? Why not see,
Far off, the shadows of his pinions dark,
And stare them from me? But no, like a spark   675
That needs must die, although its little beam
Reflects upon a diamond, my sweet dream
Fell into nothing—into stupid sleep.
And so it was, until a gentle creep,
A careful moving caught my waking ears,   680
And up I started: Ah! my sighs, my tears,
My clenched hands;—for lo! the poppies hung
Dew-dabbled on their stalks, the ouzel sung
A heavy ditty, and the sullen day
Had chidden herald Hesperus away,   685
With leaden looks: the solitary breeze
Bluster'd, and slept, and its wild self did teaze
With wayward melancholy; and r thought,
Mark me, Peona! that sometimes it brought
Faint fare-thee-wells, and sigh-shrilled adieus!—   690
Away I wander'd—all the pleasant hues
Of heaven and earth had faded: deepest shades
Were deepest dungeons; heaths and sunny glades
Were full of pestilent light; our taintless rills
Seem'd sooty, and o'er-spread with upturn'd gills   695

Of dying fish; the vermeil rose had blown
In frightful scarlet, and its thorns out-grown
Like spiked aloe. If an innocent bird
Before my heedless footsteps stirr'd, and stirr'd
In little journeys, I beheld in it   700
A disguis'd demon, missioned to knit
My soul with under darkness; to entice
My stumblings down some monstrous precipice:
Therefore I eager followed, and did curse
The disappointment. Time, that aged nurse,   705
Rock'd me to patience. Now, thank gentle heaven!
These things, with all their comfortings, are given
To my down-sunken hours, and with thee,
Sweet sister, help to stem the ebbing sea
Of weary life."

          Thus ended he, and both   710
Sat silent: for the maid was very loth
To answer; feeling well that breathed words
Would all be lost, unheard, and vain as swords
Against the enchased crocodile, or leaps
Of grasshoppers against the sun. She weeps,   715
And wonders; struggles to devise some blame;
To put on such a look as would say, Shame
On this poor weakness! but, for all her strife,
She could as soon have crush'd away the life
From a sick dove. At length, to break the pause,   720
She said with trembling chance: "Is this the cause?
This all? Yet it is strange, and sad, alas!
That one who through this middle earth should pass
Most like a sojourning demi-god, and leave
His name upon the harp-string, should achieve   725
No higher bard than simple maidenhood,
Singing alone, and fearfully,—how the blood

Left his young cheek; and how he used to stray
He knew not where; and how he would say, nay,
If any said 'twas love: and yet 'twas love;   730
What could it be but love? How a ring-dove
Let fall a sprig of yew tree in his path;
And how he died: and then, that love doth scathe,
The gentle heart, as northern blasts do roses;
And then the ballad of his sad life closes   735
With sighs, and an alas!—Endymion!
Be rather in the trumpet's mouth,—anon
Among the winds at large—that all may hearken!
Although, before the crystal heavens darken,
I watch and dote upon the silver lakes   740
Pictur'd in western cloudiness, that takes
The semblance of gold rocks and bright gold sands,
Islands, and creeks, and amber-fretted strands
With horses prancing o'er them, palaces
And towers of amethyst,—would I so tease   745
My pleasant days, because I could not mount
Into those regions? The Morphean fount
Of that fine element that visions, dreams,
And fitful whims of sleep are made of, streams
Into its airy channels with so subtle,   750
So thin a breathing, not the spider's shuttle,
Circled a million times within the space
Of a swallow's nest-door, could delay a trace,
A tinting of its quality: how light
Must dreams themselves be; seeing they're more slight   755
Than the mere nothing that engenders them![7]
Then wherefore sully the entrusted gem

---

[7] l. 747–756 This analysis of Sleep and Dream is worthy of Shakespeare, in Shakespeare's best manner.

Of high and noble life with thoughts so sick?
Why pierce high-fronted honour to the quick
For nothing but a dream?" Hereat the youth   760
Look'd up: a conflicting of shame and ruth
Was in his plaited brow: yet his eyelids
Widened a little, as when Zephyr bids
A little breeze to creep between the fans
Of careless butterflies: amid his pains   765
He seem'd to taste a drop of manna-dew,
Full palatable; and a colour grew
Upon his cheek, while thus he lifeful spake.

        "Peona! ever have I long'd to slake
My thirst for the world's praises: nothing base,   770
No merely slumberous phantasm, could unlace
The stubborn canvas for my voyage prepar'd—
Though now 'tis tatter'd; leaving my bark bar'd
And sullenly drifting: yet my higher hope
Is of too wide, too rainbow-large a scope,   775
To fret at myriads of earthly wrecks.
Wherein lies happiness? In that which becks
Our ready minds to fellowship divine,
A fellowship with essence; till we shine,
Full alchemiz'd, and free of space. Behold   780
The clear religion of heaven! Fold
A rose leaf round thy finger's taperness,
And soothe thy lips: hist, when the airy stress
Of music's kiss impregnates the free winds,
And with a sympathetic touch unbinds   785
Eolian magic from their lucid wombs:
Then old songs waken from enclouded tombs;
Old ditties sigh above their father's grave;
Ghosts of melodious prophecyings rave
Round every spot where trod Apollo's foot;   790

Bronze clarions awake, and faintly bruit,
Where long ago a giant battle was;
And, from the turf, a lullaby doth pass
In every place where infant Orpheus slept.
Feel we these things?—that moment have we stept   795
Into a sort of oneness, and our state
Is like a floating spirit's. But there are
Richer entanglements, enthralments far
More self-destroying, leading, by degrees,
To the chief intensity: the crown of these   800
Is made of love and friendship, and sits high
Upon the forehead of humanity.
All its more ponderous and bulky worth
Is friendship, whence there ever issues forth
A steady splendour; but at the tip-top,   805
There hangs by unseen film, an orbed drop
Of light, and that is love: its influence,
Thrown in our eyes, genders a novel sense,
At which we start and fret; till in the end,
Melting into its radiance, we blend,   810
Mingle, and so become a part of it,—
Nor with aught else can our souls interknit
So wingedly: when we combine therewith,
Life's self is nourish'd by its proper pith,
And we are nurtured like a pelican brood.   815
Aye, so delicious is the unsating food,
That men, who might have tower'd in the van
Of all the congregated world, to fan
And winnow from the coming step of time
All chaff of custom, wipe away all slime   820
Left by men-slugs and human serpentry,
Have been content to let occasion die,
Whilst they did sleep in love's elysium.
And, truly, I would rather be struck dumb,

Than speak against this ardent listlessness: 825
For I have ever thought that it might bless
The world with benefits unknowingly;
As does the nightingale, upperched high,
And cloister'd among cool and bunched leaves—
She sings but to her love, nor e'er conceives   830
How tiptoe Night holds back her dark-grey hood.
Just so may love, although 'tis understood
The mere commingling of passionate breath,
Produce more than our searching witnesseth:
What I know not: but who, of men, can tell   835
That flowers would bloom, or that green fruit would swell
To melting pulp, that fish would have bright mail,
The earth its dower of river, wood, and vale,
The meadows runnels, runnels pebble-stones,
The seed its harvest, or the lute its tones,   840
Tones ravishment, or ravishment its sweet,
If human souls did never kiss and greet?

   "Now, if this earthly love has power to make
Men's being mortal, immortal; to shake
Ambition from their memories, and brim   845
Their measure of content; what merest whim,
Seems all this poor endeavour after fame,
To one, who keeps within his stedfast aim
A love immortal, an immortal too.
Look not so wilder'd; for these things are true,   850
And never can be born of atomies
That buzz about our slumbers, like brain-flies,
Leaving us fancy-sick. No, no, I'm sure,
My restless spirit never could endure
To brood so long upon one luxury,   855
Unless it did, though fearfully, espy
A hope beyond the shadow of a dream.

My sayings will the less obscured seem,
When I have told thee how my waking sight
Has made me scruple whether that same night   860
Was pass'd in dreaming. Hearken, sweet Peona!
Beyond the matron-temple of Latona,
Which we should see but for these darkening boughs,
Lies a deep hollow, from whose ragged brows
Bushes and trees do lean all round athwart,   865
And meet so nearly, that with wings outraught,
And spreaded tail, a vulture could not glide
Past them, but he must brush on every side.
Some moulder'd steps lead into this cool cell,
Far as the slabbed margin of a well,   870
Whose patient level peeps its crystal eye
Right upward, through the bushes, to the sky.
Oft have I brought thee flowers, on their stalks set
Like vestal primroses, but dark velvet
Edges them round, and they have golden pits: 875
'Twas there I got them, from the gaps and slits
In a mossy stone, that sometimes was my seat,
When all above was faint with mid-day heat.
And there in strife no burning thoughts to heed,
I'd bubble up the water through a reed;   880
So reaching back to boy-hood: make me ships
Of moulted feathers, touchwood, alder chips,
With leaves stuck in them; and the Neptune be
Of their petty ocean. Oftener, heavily,
When love-lorn hours had left me less a child,   885
I sat contemplating the figures wild
Of o'er-head clouds melting the mirror through.
Upon a day, while thus I watch'd, by flew
A cloudy Cupid, with his bow and quiver;
So plainly character'd, no breeze would shiver   890
The happy chance: so happy, I was fain

To follow it upon the open plain,
And, therefore, was just going; when, behold!
A wonder, fair as any I have told—
The same bright face I tasted in my sleep,   895
Smiling in the clear well. My heart did leap
Through the cool depth.—It moved as if to flee—
I started up, when lo! refreshfully,
There came upon my face, in plenteous showers,
Dew-drops, and dewy buds, and leaves, and flowers,   900
Wrapping all objects from my smothered sight,
Bathing my spirit in a new delight.
Aye, such a breathless honey-feel of bliss
Alone preserved me from the drear abyss
Of death, for the fair form had gone again.   905
Pleasure is oft a visitant; but pain
Clings cruelly to us, like the gnawing sloth
On the deer's tender haunches: late, and loth,
'Tis scar'd away by slow returning pleasure.
How sickening, how dark the dreadful leisure   910
Of weary days, made deeper exquisite,
By a fore-knowledge of unslumbrous night!
Like sorrow came upon me, heavier still,
Than when I wander'd from the poppy hill:
And a whole age of lingering moments crept   915
Sluggishly by, ere more contentment swept
Away at once the deadly yellow spleen.
Yes, thrice have I this fair enchantment seen;
Once more been tortured with renewed life.
When last the wintry gusts gave over strife   920
With the conquering sun of spring, and left the skies
Warm and serene, but yet with moistened eyes
In pity of the shatter'd infant buds,—
That time thou didst adorn, with amber studs,
My hunting cap, because I laugh'd and smil'd,   925

39

Chatted with thee, and many days exil'd
All torment from my breast;—'twas even then,
Straying about, yet, coop'd up in the den
Of helpless discontent,—hurling my lance
From place to place, and following at chance,   930
At last, by hap, through some young trees it struck,
And, plashing among bedded pebbles, stuck
In the middle of a brook,—whose silver ramble
Down twenty little falls, through reeds and bramble,
Tracing along, it brought me to a cave,   935
Whence it ran brightly forth, and white did lave
The nether sides of mossy stones and rock,—
'Mong which it gurgled blythe adieus, to mock
Its own sweet grief at parting. Overhead,
Hung a lush screen of drooping weeds, and spread   940
Thick, as to curtain up some wood-nymph's home.
"Ah! impious mortal, whither do I roam?"
Said I, low voic'd: "Ah whither! 'Tis the grot
Of Proserpine, when Hell, obscure and hot,
Doth her resign; and where her tender hands   945
She dabbles, on the cool and sluicy sands:
Or 'tis the cell of Echo, where she sits,
And babbles thorough silence, till her wits
Are gone in tender madness, and anon,
Faints into sleep, with many a dying tone   950
Of sadness. O that she would take my vows,
And breathe them sighingly among the boughs,
To sue her gentle ears for whose fair head,
Daily, I pluck sweet flowerets from their bed,
And weave them dyingly—send honey-whispers   955
Round every leaf, that all those gentle lispers
May sigh my love unto her pitying!
O charitable echo! hear, and sing
This ditty to her!—tell her"—so I stay'd

My foolish tongue, and listening, half afraid,   960
Stood stupefied with my own empty folly,
And blushing for the freaks of melancholy.
Salt tears were coming, when I heard my name
Most fondly lipp'd, and then these accents came:
'Endymion! the cave is secreter   965
Than the isle of Delos. Echo hence shall stir
No sighs but sigh-warm kisses, or light noise
Of thy combing hand, the while it travelling cloys
And trembles through my labyrinthine hair."
At that oppress'd I hurried in.—Ah! where   970
Are those swift moments? Whither are they fled?
I'll smile no more, Peona; nor will wed
Sorrow the way to death, but patiently
Bear up against it: so farewel, sad sigh;
And come instead demurest meditation,   975
To occupy me wholly, and to fashion
My pilgrimage for the world's dusky brink.
No more will I count over, link by link,
My chain of grief: no longer strive to find
A half-forgetfulness in mountain wind   980
Blustering about my ears: aye, thou shalt see,
Dearest of sisters, what my life shall be;
What a calm round of hours shall make my days.
There is a paly flame of hope that plays
Where'er I look: but yet, I'll say 'tis naught—   985
And here I bid it die. Have not I caught,
Already, a more healthy countenance?
By this the sun is setting; we may chance
Meet some of our near-dwellers with my car."

   This said, he rose, faint-smiling like a star   990
Through autumn mists, and took Peona's hand:
They stept into the boat, and launch'd from land.

41

Endymion

BOOK II

O SOVEREIGN power of love! O grief! O balm!
All records, saving thine, come cool, and calm,
And shadowy, through the mist of passed years:
For others, good or bad, hatred and tears
Have become indolent; but touching thine,   5
One sigh doth echo, one poor sob doth pine,
One kiss brings honey-dew from buried days.
The woes of Troy, towers smothering o'er their blaze,
Stiff-holden shields, far-piercing spears, keen blades,
Struggling, and blood, and shrieks—all dimly fades   10
Into some backward corner of the brain;
Yet, in our very souls, we feel amain
The close of Troilus and Cressid sweet.
Hence, pageant history! hence, gilded cheat!
Swart planet in the universe of deeds!   15
Wide sea, that one continuous murmur breeds
Along the pebbled shore of memory!
Many old rotten-timber'd boats there be
Upon thy vaporous bosom, magnified
To goodly vessels; many a sail of pride,   20
And golden keel'd, is left unlaunch'd and dry.
But wherefore this? What care, though owl did fly
About the great Athenian admiral's mast?
What care, though striding Alexander past
The Indus with his Macedonian numbers?   25
Though old Ulysses tortured from his slumbers
The glutted Cyclops, what care?—Juliet leaning
Amid her window-flowers,—sighing,—weaning

Tenderly her fancy from its maiden snow,
Doth more avail than these: the silver flow   30
Of Hero's tears, the swoon of Imogen,
Fair Pastorella in the bandit's den,
Are things to brood on with more ardency
Than the death-day of empires. Fearfully
Must such conviction come upon his head,   35
Who, thus far, discontent, has dared to tread,
Without one muse's smile, or kind behest,
The path of love and poesy.¹ But rest,
In chaffing² restlessness, is yet more drear
Than to be crush'd, in striving to uprear   40
Love's standard on the battlements of song.
So once more days and nights aid me along,
Like legion'd soldiers.

                    Brain-sick shepherd-prince,
What promise hast thou faithful guarded since
The day of sacrifice? Or, have new sorrows   45
Come with the constant dawn upon thy morrows?
Alas! 'tis his old grief. For many days,
Has he been wandering in uncertain ways:
Through wilderness, and woods of mossed oaks;
Counting his woe-worn minutes, by the strokes   50
Of the lone woodcutter; and listening still,
Hour after hour, to each lush-leav'd rill.
Now he is sitting by a shady spring,
And elbow-deep with feverous fingering
Stems the upbursting cold: a wild rose tree   55
Pavilions him in bloom, and he doth see
A bud which snares his fancy: lo! but now

---

¹ l. 34–38 Keats here alludes to the ill-success of his volume of 1817.
² l. 39 "chaffing": chafing.

He plucks it, dips its stalk in the water: how!
It swells, it buds, it flowers beneath his sight;
And, in the middle, there is softly pight³   60
A golden butterfly; upon whose wings
There must be surely character'd strange things,
For with wide eye he wonders, and smiles oft.

    Lightly this little herald flew aloft,
Follow'd by glad Endymion's clasped hands: 65
Onward it flies. From languor's sullen bands
His limbs are loos'd, and eager, on he hies
Dazzled to trace it in the sunny skies.
It seem'd he flew, the way so easy was;
And like a new-born spirit did he pass   70
Through the green evening quiet in the sun,
O'er many a heath, through many a woodland dun,
Through buried paths, where sleepy twilight dreams
The summer time away. One track unseams
A wooded cleft, and, far away, the blue   75
Of ocean fades upon him; then, anew,
He sinks adown a solitary glen,
Where there was never sound of mortal men,
Saving, perhaps, some snow-light cadences
Melting to silence, when upon the breeze   80
Some holy bark let forth an anthem sweet,
To cheer itself to Delphi. Still his feet
Went swift beneath the merry-winged guide,
Until it reached a splashing fountain's side
That, near a cavern's mouth, for ever pour'd   85
Unto the temperate air: then high it soar'd,
And, downward, suddenly began to dip,
As if, athirst with so much toil, 'twould sip

---

³ l. 60 "pight": placed.

The crystal spout-head: so it did, with touch
Most delicate, as though afraid to smutch   90
Even with mealy gold the waters clear.
But, at that very touch, to disappear
So fairy-quick, was strange! Bewildered,
Endymion sought around, and shook each bed
Of covert flowers in vain; and then he flung   95
Himself along the grass. What gentle tongue,
What whisperer disturb'd his gloomy rest?
It was a nymph uprisen to the breast
In the fountain's pebbly margin, and she stood
'Mong lilies, like the youngest of the brood.   100
To him her dripping hand she softly kist,
And anxiously began to plait and twist
Her ringlets round her fingers, saying: "Youth!
Too long, alas, hast thou starv'd on the ruth,
The bitterness of love: too long indeed,   105
Seeing thou art so gentle. Could I weed
Thy soul of care, by heavens, I would offer
All the bright riches of my crystal coffer
To Amphitrite; all my clear-eyed fish,
Golden, or rainbow-sided, or purplish,   110
Vermilion-tail'd, or finn'd with silvery gauze;
Yea, or my veined pebble-floor, that draws
A virgin light to the deep; my grotto-sands
Tawny and gold, ooz'd slowly from far lands
By my diligent springs; my level lilies, shells,   115
My charming rod, my potent river spells;
Yes, every thing, even to the pearly cup
Meander gave me,—for I bubbled up
To fainting creatures in a desert wild.
But woe is me, I am but as a child   120
To gladden thee; and all I dare to say,
Is, that I pity thee; that on this day

I've been thy guide; that thou must wander far
In other regions, past the scanty bar
To mortal steps, before thou cans't be ta'en   125
From every wasting sigh, from every pain,
Into the gentle bosom of thy love.
Why it is thus, one knows in heaven above:
But, a poor Naiad, I guess not. Farewel!
I have a ditty for my hollow cell."   130

    Hereat, she vanished from Endymion's gaze,
Who brooded o'er the water in amaze:
The dashing fount pour'd on, and where its pool
Lay, half asleep, in grass and rushes cool,
Quick waterflies and gnats were sporting still,   135
And fish were dimpling, as if good nor ill
Had fallen out that hour. The wanderer,
Holding his forehead, to keep off the burr
Of smothering fancies, patiently sat down;
And, while beneath the evening's sleepy frown   140
Glow-worms began to trim their starry lamps,
Thus breath'd he to himself: "Whoso encamps
To take a fancied city of delight,
O what a wretch is he! and when 'tis his,
After long toil and travelling, to miss   145
The kernel of his hopes, how more than vile:
Yet, for him there's refreshment even in toil;
Another city doth he set about,
Free from the smallest pebble-bead of doubt
That he will seize on trickling honey-combs: 150
Alas, he finds them dry; and then he foams,
And onward to another city speeds.
But this is human life: the war, the deeds,
The disappointment, the anxiety,
Imagination's struggles, far and nigh,   155

All human; bearing in themselves this good,
That they are sill the air, the subtle food,
To make us feel existence, and to shew
How quiet death is. Where soil is men grow,
Whether to weeds or flowers; but for me,   160
There is no depth to strike in: I can see
Nought earthly worth my compassing; so stand
Upon a misty, jutting head of land—
Alone? No, no; and by the Orphean lute,
When mad Eurydice is listening to 't;   165
I'd rather stand upon this misty peak,
With not a thing to sigh for, or to seek,
But the soft shadow of my thrice-seen love,
Than be—I care not what. O meekest dove
Of heaven! O Cynthia, ten-times bright and fair!   170
From thy blue throne, now filling all the air,
Glance but one little beam of temper'd light
Into my bosom, that the dreadful might
And tyranny of love be somewhat scar'd!
Yet do not so, sweet queen; one torment spar'd,   175
Would give a pang to jealous misery,
Worse than the torment's self: but rather tie
Large wings upon my shoulders, and point out
My love's far dwelling. Though the playful rout
Of Cupids shun thee, too divine art thou,   180
Too keen in beauty, for thy silver prow
Not to have dipp'd in love's most gentle stream.
O be propitious, nor severely deem
My madness impious; for, by all the stars
That tend thy bidding, I do think the bars   185
That kept my spirit in are burst—that I
Am sailing with thee through the dizzy sky!
How beautiful thou art! The world how deep!
How tremulous-dazzlingly the wheels sweep

Around their axle! Then these gleaming reins,   190
How lithe! When this thy chariot attains
Is airy goal, haply some bower veils
Those twilight eyes? Those eyes!—my spirit fails—
Dear goddess, help! or the wide-gaping air
Will gulph me—help!"—At this with madden'd stare,   195
And lifted hands, and trembling lips he stood;
Like old Deucalion mountain'd o'er the flood,
Or blind Orion hungry for the morn.
And, but from the deep cavern there was borne
A voice, he had been froze to senseless stone;   200
Nor sigh of his, nor plaint, nor passion'd moan
Had more been heard. Thus swell'd it forth: "Descend,
Young mountaineer! descend where alleys bend
Into the sparry hollows of the world!
Oft hast thou seen bolts of the thunder hurl'd   205
As from thy threshold, day by day hast been
A little lower than the chilly sheen
Of icy pinnacles, and dipp'dst thine arms
Into the deadening ether that still charms
Their marble being: now, as deep profound   210
As those are high, descend! He ne'er is crown'd
With immortality, who fears to follow
Where airy voices lead: so through the hollow,
The silent mysteries of earth, descend!"

He heard but the last words, nor could contend   215
One moment in reflection: for he fled
Into the fearful deep, to hide his head
From the clear moon, the trees, and coming madness.

'Twas far too strange, and wonderful for sadness;
Sharpening, by degrees, his appetite   220
To dive into the deepest. Dark, nor light,

The region; nor bright, nor sombre wholly,
But mingled up; a gleaming melancholy;
A dusky empire and its diadems;
One faint eternal eventide of gems.   225
Aye, millions sparkled on a vein of gold,
Along whose track the prince quick footsteps told,
With all its lines abrupt and angular:
Out-shooting sometimes, like a meteor-star,
Through a vast antre; then the metal woof,   230
Like Vulcan's rainbow, with some monstrous roof
Curves hugely: now, far in the deep abyss,
It seems an angry lightning, and doth hiss
Fancy into belief: anon it leads
Through winding passages, where sameness breeds   235
Vexing conceptions of some sudden change;
Whether to silver grots, or giant range
Of sapphire columns, or fantastic bridge
Athwart a flood of crystal. On a ridge
Now fareth he, that o'er the vast beneath   240
Towers like an ocean-cliff, and whence he seeth
A hundred waterfalls, whose voices come
But as the murmuring surge. Chilly and numb
His bosom grew, when first he, far away,
Descried an orbed diamond, set to fray   245
Old darkness from his throne: 'twas like the sun
Uprisen o'er chaos: and with such a stun
Came the amazement, that, absorb'd in it,
He saw not fiercer wonders—past the wit
Of any spirit to tell, but one of those   250
Who, when this planet's sphering time doth close,
Will be its high remembrancers: who they?
The mighty ones who have made eternal day
For Greece and England. While astonishment
With deep-drawn sighs was quieting, he went   255

Into a marble gallery, passing through
A mimic temple, so complete and true
In sacred custom, that he well nigh fear'd
To search it inwards, whence far off appear'd,
Through a long pillar'd vista, a fair shrine,   260
And, just beyond, on light tiptoe divine,
A quiver'd Dian. Stepping awfully,
The youth approach'd; oft turning his veil'd eye
Down sidelong aisles, and into niches old.
And when, more near against the marble cold   265
He had touch'd his forehead, he began to thread
All courts and passages, where silence dead
Rous'd by his whispering footsteps murmured faint:
And long he travers'd to and fro, to acquaint
Himself with every mystery, and awe;   270
Till, weary, he sat down before the maw
Of a wide outlet, fathomless and dim
To wild uncertainty and shadows grim.
There, when new wonders ceas'd to float before,
And thoughts of self came on, how crude and sore   275
The journey homeward to habitual self!
A mad-pursuing of the fog-born elf,
Whose flitting lantern, through rude nettle-briar,
Cheats us into a swamp, into a fire,
Into the bosom of a hated thing.   280

    What misery most drowningly doth sing
In lone Endymion's ear, now he has caught
The goal of consciousness? Ah, 'tis the thought,
The deadly feel of solitude: for lo!
He cannot see the heavens, nor the flow   285
Of rivers, nor hill-flowers running wild
In pink and purple chequer, nor, up-pil'd,
The cloudy rack slow journeying in the west,

Like herded elephants; nor felt, nor prest
Cool grass, nor tasted the fresh slumberous air;   290
But far from such companionship to wear
An unknown time, surcharg'd with grief, away,
Was now his lot. And must he patient stay,
Tracing fantastic figures with his spear?
"No!" exclaimed he, "why should I tarry here?"   295
No! loudly echoed times innumerable.
At which he straightway started, and 'gan tell
His paces back into the temple's chief;
Warming and glowing strong in the belief
Of help from Dian: so that when again   300
He caught her airy form, thus did he plain,
Moving more near the while. "O Haunter chaste
Of river sides, and woods, and heathy waste,
Where with thy silver bow and arrows keen
Art thou now forested? O woodland Queen,   305
What smoothest air thy smoother forehead woos?
Where dost thou listen to the wide halloos
Of thy disparted nymphs? Through what dark tree
Glimmers thy crescent? Wheresoe'er it be,
'Tis in the breath of heaven: thou dost taste   310
Freedom as none can taste it, nor dost waste
Thy loveliness in dismal elements;
But, finding in our green earth sweet contents,
There livest blissfully. Ah, if to thee
It feels Elysian, how rich to me,   315
An exil'd mortal, sounds its pleasant name!
Within my breast there lives a choking flame—
O let me cool it among the zephyr-boughs!⁴

---

⁴ l. 318 "zephyr-boughs among," the common reading here, was probably in the
mind of Keats. But with a poet of literary training so incomplete, so
unconventional, and of such imaginative force, conjectural emendation, to which

51

A homeward fever parches up my tongue—
O let me slake it at the running springs!　　　　320
Upon my ear a noisy nothing rings—
O let me once more hear the linnet's note!
Before mine eyes thick films and shadows float—
O let me 'noint them with the heaven's light!
Dost thou now lave thy feet and ankles white?　　325
O think how sweet to me the freshening sluice!
Dost thou now please thy thirst with berry-juice?
O think how this dry palate would rejoice!
If in soft slumber thou dost hear my voice,
Oh think how I should love a bed of flowers!—　　330
Young goddess! let me see my native bowers!
Deliver me from this rapacious deep!"

　　Thus ending loudly, as he would o'erleap
His destiny, alert he stood: but when
Obstinate silence came heavily again,　　　　335
Feeling about for its old couch of space
And airy cradle, lowly bow'd his face
Desponding, o'er the marble floor's cold thrill.
But 'twas not long; for, sweeter than the rill
To its old channel, or a swollen tide　　　　340
To margin sallows, were the leaves he spied,
And flowers, and wreaths, and ready myrtle crowns
Up heaping through the slab: refreshment drowns
Itself, and strives its own delights to hide—
Nor in one spot alone; the floral pride　　　　345
In a long whispering birth enchanted grew

---

his abnormal phrases and rhythms tempt, is even more than ordinarily uncertain and undesirable.—The verbal peculiarities of Keats I have hence, also, in general left unnoticed. He copied much, no doubt, from our elder poets: but he also invents with the freedom which is one of the prerogatives of all Poetry, and of all language in a vital condition.

Before his footsteps; as when heav'd anew
Old ocean rolls a lengthened wave to the shore,
Down whose green back the short-liv'd foam, all hoar,
Bursts gradual, with a wayward indolence.   350

    Increasing still in heart, and pleasant sense,
Upon his fairy journey on he hastes;
So anxious for the end, he scarcely wastes
One moment with his hand among the sweets:
Onward he goes—he stops—his bosom beats   355
As plainly in his ear, as the faint charm
Of which the throbs were born. This still alarm,
This sleepy music, forc'd him walk tiptoe:
For it came more softly than the east could blow
Arion's magic to the Atlantic isles;   360
Or than the west, made jealous by the smiles
Of thron'd Apollo, could breathe back the lyre
To seas Ionian and Tyrian.

    O did he ever live, that lonely man,
Who lov'd—and music slew not? 'Tis the pest   365
Of love, that fairest joys give most unrest;
That things of delicate and tenderest worth
Are swallow'd all, and made a seared dearth,
By one consuming flame: it doth immerse
And suffocate true blessings in a curse.   370
Half-happy, by comparison of bliss,
Is miserable. 'Twas even so with this
Dew-dropping melody, in the Carian's ear;
First heaven, then hell, and then forgotten clear,
Vanish'd in elemental passion.   375

    And down some swart abysm he had gone,
Had not a heavenly guide benignant led

To where thick myrtle branches, 'gainst his head
Brushing, awakened: then the sounds again
Went noiseless as a passing noontide rain   380
Over a bower, where little space he stood;
For as the sunset peeps into a wood
So saw he panting light, and towards it went
Through winding alleys; and lo, wonderment!
Upon soft verdure saw, one here, one there,   385
Cupids a slumbering on their pinions fair.

    After a thousand mazes overgone,
At last, with sudden step, he came upon
A chamber, myrtle wall'd, embowered high,
Full of light, incense, tender minstrelsy,   390
And more of beautiful and strange beside:
For on a silken couch of rosy pride,
In midst of all, there lay a sleeping youth
Of fondest beauty; fonder, in fair sooth,
Than sighs could fathom, or contentment reach: 395
And coverlids gold-tinted like the peach,
Or ripe October's faded marigolds,
Fell sleek about him in a thousand folds—
Not hiding up an Apollonian curve
Of neck and shoulder, nor the tenting[5] swerve   400
Of knee from knee, nor ankles pointing light;
But rather, giving them to the filled sight
Officiously. Sideway his face repos'd
On one white arm, and tenderly unclos'd,
By tenderest pressure, a faint damask mouth   405
To slumbery pout; just as the morning south
Disparts a dew-lipp'd rose. Above his head,

---

[5] l. 400 *tenting*: perhaps, (it has been suggested to me), referring to the drapery of Adonis, stretched from knee to knee.

Four lily stalks did their white honours wed
To make a coronal; and round him grew
All tendrils green, of every bloom and hue,   410
Together intertwin'd and trammel'd fresh:
The vine of glossy sprout; the ivy mesh,
Shading its Ethiop berries; and woodbine,
Of velvet leaves and bugle-blooms divine;
Convolvulus in streaked vases flush;   415
The creeper, mellowing for an autumn blush;
And virgin's bower, trailing airily;
With others of the sisterhood. Hard by,
Stood serene Cupids watching silently.
One, kneeling to a lyre, touch'd the strings,   420
Muffling to death the pathos with his wings;
And, ever and anon, uprose to look
At the youth's slumber; while another took
A willow-bough, distilling odorous dew,
And shook it on his hair; another flew   425
In through the woven roof, and fluttering-wise
Rain'd violets upon his sleeping eyes.

    At these enchantments, and yet many more,
The breathless Latmian wonder'd o'er and o'er;
Until, impatient in embarrassment,   430
He forthright pass'd, and lightly treading went
To that same feather'd lyrist, who straightway,
Smiling, thus whisper'd: "Though from upper day
Thou art a wanderer, and thy presence here
Might seem unholy, be of happy cheer!   435
For 'tis the nicest touch of human honour,
When some ethereal and high-favouring donor
Presents immortal bowers to mortal sense;
As now 'tis done to thee, Endymion. Hence
Was I in no wise startled. So recline   440

Upon these living flowers. Here is wine,
Alive with sparkles—never, I aver,
Since Ariadne was a vintager,[6]
So cool a purple: taste these juicy pears,
Sent me by sad Vertumnus,[7] when his fears   445
Were high about Pomona: here is cream,
Deepening to richness from a snowy gleam;
Sweeter than that nurse Amalthea skimm'd
For the boy Jupiter: and here, undimm'd
By any touch, a bunch of blooming plums   450
Ready to melt between an infant's gums:
And here is manna pick'd from Syrian trees,
In starlight, by the three Hesperides.
Feast on, and meanwhile I will let thee know
Of all these things around us." He did so,   455
Still brooding o'er the cadence of his lyre;
And thus: "I need not any hearing tire
By telling how the sea-born goddess pin'd
For a mortal youth, and how she strove to bind
Him all in all unto her doting self.   460
Who would not be so prison'd? but, fond elf,
He was content to let her amorous plea
Faint through his careless arms; content to see
An unseiz'd heaven dying at his feet;
Content, O fool! to make a cold retreat,   465
When on the pleasant grass such love, lovelorn,
Lay sorrowing; when every tear was born
Of diverse passion; when her lips and eyes
Were clos'd in sullen moisture, and quick sighs
Came vex'd and pettish through her nostrils small.   470

---

[6] l. 443 Since Ariadne became companion to Dionysos.
[7] l. 445 *Vertumnus:* This name, with *Pomona,* after the fashion of the Italian Renaissance, carries us abruptly from Hellenic to Graeco-Roman mythology.— The Cupid picture (l. 506) is classical, but in a similar vein.

Hush! no exclaim—yet, justly mightst thou call
Curses upon his head.—I was half glad,
But my poor mistress went distract and mad,
When the boar tusk'd him: so away she flew
To Jove's high throne, and by her plainings drew   475
Immortal tear-drops down the thunderer's beard;
Whereon, it was decreed he should be rear'd
Each summer time to life. Lo! this is he,
That same Adonis, safe in the privacy
Of this still region all his winter-sleep.   480
Aye, sleep; for when our love-sick queen did weep
Over his waned corse, the tremulous shower
Heal'd up the wound, and, with a balmy power,
Medicined death to a lengthened drowsiness:
The which she fills with visions, and doth dress   485
In all this quiet luxury; and hath set
Us young immortals, without any let,
To watch his slumber through. 'Tis well nigh pass'd,
Even to a moment's filling up, and fast
She scuds with summer breezes, to pant through   490
The first long kiss, warm firstling, to renew
Embower'd sports in Cytherea's isle.
Look! how those winged listeners all this while
Stand anxious: see! behold!"—This clamant word
Broke through the careful silence; for they heard   495
A rustling noise of leaves, and out there flutter'd
Pigeons and doves: Adonis something mutter'd,
The while one hand, that erst upon his thigh
Lay dormant, mov'd convuls'd and gradually
Up to his forehead. Then there was a hum   500
Of sudden voices, echoing, "Come! come!
Arise! awake! Clear summer has forth walk'd
Unto the clover-sward, and she has talk'd
Full soothingly to every nested finch:

Rise, Cupids! or we'll give the blue-bell pinch   505
To your dimpled arms. Once more sweet life begin!"
At this, from every side they hurried in,
Rubbing their sleepy eyes with lazy wrists,
And doubling overhead their little fists
In backward yawns. But all were soon alive: 510
For as delicious wine doth, sparkling, dive
In nectar'd clouds and curls through water fair,
So from the arbour roof down swell'd an air
Odorous and enlivening; making all
To laugh, and play, and sing, and loudly call   515
For their sweet queen: when lo! the wreathed green
Disparted, and far upward could be seen
Blue heaven, and a silver car, air-borne,
Whose silent wheels, fresh wet from clouds of morn,
Spun off a drizzling dew,—which falling chill   520
On soft Adonis' shoulders, made him still
Nestle and turn uneasily about.
Soon were the white doves plain, with necks stretch'd out,
And silken traces lighten'd in descent;
And soon, returning from love's banishment,   525
Queen Venus leaning downward open arm'd:
Her shadow fell upon his breast, and charm'd
A tumult to his heart, and a new life
Into his eyes. Ah, miserable strife,
But for her comforting! unhappy sight,   530
But meeting her blue orbs! Who, who can write
Of these first minutes? The unchariest muse
To embracements warm as theirs makes coy excuse.

    O it has ruffled every spirit there,
Saving love's self, who stands superb to share   535
The general gladness: awfully he stands;
A sovereign quell is in his waving hands;

No sight can bear the lightning of his bow;
His quiver is mysterious, none can know
What themselves think of it; from forth his eyes   540
There darts strange light of varied hues and dyes:
A scowl is sometimes on his brow, but who
Look full upon it feel anon the blue
Of his fair eyes run liquid through their souls.
Endymion feels it, and no more controls   545
The burning prayer within him; so, bent low,
He had begun a plaining of his woe.
But Venus, bending forward, said: "My child,
Favour this gentle youth; his days are wild
With love—he—but alas! too well I see   550
Thou know'st the deepness of his misery.
Ah, smile not so, my son: I tell thee true,
That when through heavy hours I used to rue
The endless sleep of this new-born Adon',
This stranger ay I pitied. For upon   555
A dreary morning once I fled away
Into the breezy clouds, to weep and pray
For this my love: for vexing Mars had teaz'd
Me even to tears: thence, when a little eas'd,
Down-looking, vacant, through a hazy wood,   560
I saw this youth as he despairing stood:
Those same dark curls blown vagrant in the wind:
Those same full fringed lids a constant blind
Over his sullen eyes: I saw him throw
Himself on wither'd leaves, even as though   565
Death had come sudden; for no jot he mov'd,
Yet mutter'd wildly. I could hear he lov'd
Some fair immortal, and that his embrace
Had zoned her through the night. There is no trace
Of this in heaven: I have mark'd each cheek,   570
And find it is the vainest thing to seek;

And that of all things 'tis kept secretest.
Endymion! one day thou wilt be blest:
So still obey the guiding hand that fends
Thee safely through these wonders for sweet ends.   575
'Tis a concealment needful in extreme;
And if I guess'd not so, the sunny beam
Thou shouldst mount up to with me. Now adieu!
Here must we leave thee."—At these words up flew
The impatient doves, up rose the floating car,   580
Up went the hum celestial. High afar
The Latmian saw them minish into nought;
And, when all were clear vanish'd, still he caught
A vivid lightning from that dreadful bow.
When all was darkened, with Etnean throe   585
The earth clos'd—gave a solitary moan—
And left him once again in twilight lone.

   He did not rave, he did not stare aghast,
For all those visions were o'ergone, and past,
And he in loneliness: he felt assur'd   590
Of happy times, when all he had endur'd
Would seem a feather to the mighty prize.
So, with unusual gladness, on he hies
Through caves, and palaces of mottled ore,
Gold dome, and crystal wall, and turquois floor,   595
Black polish'd porticos of awful shade,
And, at the last, a diamond balustrade,
Leading afar past wild magnificence,
Spiral through ruggedest loopholes, and thence
Stretching across a void, then guiding o'er   600
Enormous chasms, where, all foam and roar,
Streams subterranean tease their granite beds;
Then heighten'd just above the silvery heads
Of a thousand fountains, so that he could dash

The waters with his spear; but at the splash,   605
Done heedlessly, those spouting columns rose
Sudden a poplar's height, and 'gan to enclose
His diamond path with fretwork, streaming round
Alive, and dazzling cool, and with a sound,
Haply, like dolphin tumults, when sweet shells   610
Welcome the float of Thetis. Long he dwells
On this delight; for, every minute's space,
The streams with changed magic interlace:
Sometimes like delicatest lattices,
Cover'd with crystal vines; then weeping trees,   615
Moving about as in a gentle wind,
Which, in a wink, to watery gauze refin'd,
Pour'd into shapes of curtain'd canopies,
Spangled, and rich with liquid broideries
Of flowers, peacocks, swans, and naiads fair.   620
Swifter than lightning went these wonders rare;
And then the water, into stubborn streams
Collecting, mimick'd the wrought oaken beams,
Pillars, and frieze, and high fantastic roof,
Of those dusk places in times far aloof   625
Cathedrals call'd. He bade a loth farewel
To these founts Protean, passing gulph, and dell,
And torrent, and ten thousand jutting shapes,
Half seen through deepest gloom, and griesly gapes,
Blackening on every side, and overhead   630
A vaulted dome like Heaven's, far bespread
With starlight gems: aye, all so huge and strange,
The solitary felt a hurried change
Working within him into something dreary,—
Vex'd like a morning eagle, lost, and weary,   635
And purblind amid foggy, midnight wolds.
But he revives at once: for who beholds
New sudden things, nor casts his mental slough?

Forth from a rugged arch, in the dusk below,
Came mother Cybele! alone—alone—   640
In sombre chariot; dark foldings thrown
About her majesty, and front death-pale,
With turrets crown'd. Four maned lions hale
The sluggish wheels; solemn their toothed maws,
Their surly eyes brow-hidden, heavy paws   645
Uplifted drowsily, and nervy tails
Cowering their tawny brushes. Silent sails
This shadowy queen athwart, and faints away
In another gloomy arch.

                Wherefore delay,
Young traveller, in such a mournful place?   650
Art thou wayworn, or canst not further trace
The diamond path? And does it indeed end
Abrupt in middle air? Yet earthward bend
Thy forehead, and to Jupiter cloud-borne
Call ardently! He was indeed wayworn;   655
Abrupt, in middle air, his way was lost;
To cloud-borne Jove he bowed, and there crost
Towards him a large eagle, 'twixt whose wings,
Without one impious word, himself he flings,
Committed to the darkness and the gloom: 660
Down, down, uncertain to what pleasant doom,
Swift as a fathoming plummet down he fell
Through unknown things; till exhaled asphodel,
And rose, with spicy fannings interbreath'd,
Came swelling forth where little caves were wreath'd 665
So thick with leaves and mosses, that they seem'd
Large honey-combs of green, and freshly teem'd
With airs delicious. In the greenest nook
The eagle landed him, and farewel took.
    It was a jasmine bower, all bestrown   670

62

With golden moss. His every sense had grown
Ethereal for pleasure; 'bove his head
Flew a delight half-graspable; his tread
Was Hesperean; to his capable ears
Silence was music from the holy spheres;   675
A dewy luxury was in his eyes;
The little flowers felt his pleasant sighs
And stirr'd them faintly. Verdant cave and cell
He wander'd through, oft wondering at such swell
Of sudden exaltation: but, "Alas!   680
Said he, "will all this gush of feeling pass
Away in solitude? And must they wane,
Like melodies upon a sandy plain,
Without an echo? Then shall I be left
So sad, so melancholy, so bereft!   685
Yet still I feel immortal! O my love,
My breath of life, where art thou? High above,
Dancing before the morning gates of heaven?
Or keeping watch among those starry seven,
Old Atlas' children? Art a maid of the waters,   690
One of shell-winding Triton's bright-hair'd daughters?
Or art, impossible! a nymph of Dian's,
Weaving a coronal of tender scions
For very idleness? Where'er thou art,
Methinks it now is at my will to start   695
Into thine arms; to scare Aurora's train,
And snatch thee from the morning; o'er the main
To scud like a wild bird, and take thee off
From thy sea-foamy cradle; or to doff
Thy shepherd vest, and woo thee mid fresh leaves.   700
No, no, too eagerly my soul deceives
Its powerless self: I know this cannot be.
O let me then by some sweet dreaming flee
To her entrancements: hither sleep awhile!

Hither most gentle sleep! and soothing foil   705
For some few hours the coming solitude."

   Thus spake he, and that moment felt endued
With power to dream deliciously; so wound
Through a dim passage, searching till he found
The smoothest mossy bed and deepest, where   710
He threw himself, and just into the air
Stretching his indolent arms, he took, O bliss!
A naked waist: "Fair Cupid, whence is this?"
A well-known voice sigh'd, "Sweetest, here am I!"
At which soft ravishment, with doating cry   715
They trembled to each other.—Helicon!
O fountain'd hill! Old Homer's Helicon!
That thou wouldst spout a little streamlet o'er
These sorry pages; then the verse would soar
And sing above this gentle pair, like lark   720
Over his nested young: but all is dark
Around thine aged top, and thy clear fount
Exhales in mists to heaven. Aye, the count
Of mighty Poets is made up; the scroll
Is folded by the Muses; the bright roll   725
Is in Apollo's hand: our dazed eyes
Have seen a new tinge in the western skies:
The world has done its duty. Yet, oh yet,
Although the sun of poesy is set,
These lovers did embrace, and we must weep   730
That there is no old power left to steep
A quill immortal in their joyous tears.
Long time in silence did their anxious fears
Question that thus it was; long time they lay
Fondling and kissing every doubt away;   735
Long time ere soft caressing sobs began
To mellow into words, and then there ran

Two bubbling springs of talk from their sweet lips.
"O known Unknown! from whom my being sips
Such darling essence, wherefore may I not   740
Be ever in these arms? in this sweet spot
Pillow my chin for ever? ever press
These toying hands and kiss their smooth excess?
Why not for ever and for ever feel
That breath about my eyes? Ah, thou wilt steal   745
Away from me again, indeed, indeed—
Thou wilt be gone away, and wilt not heed
My lonely madness. Speak, my kindest fair!
Is—is it to be so? No! Who will dare
To pluck thee from me? And, of thine own will,   750
Full well I feel thou wouldst not leave me. Still
Let me entwine thee surer, surer—now
How can we part? Elysium! who art thou?
Who, that thou canst not be for ever here,
Or lift me with thee to some starry sphere?   755
Enchantress! tell me by this soft embrace,
By the most soft completion of thy face,
Those lips, O slippery blisses, twinkling eyes,
And by these tenderest, milky sovereignties—
These tenderest, and by the nectar-wine,   760
The passion"————"O lov'd Ida the divine![8]
Endymion! dearest! Ah, unhappy me!
His soul will 'scape us—O felicity!
How he does love me! His poor temples beat
To the very tune of love—how sweet, sweet, sweet.   765
Revive, dear youth, or I shall faint and die;
Revive, or these soft hours will hurry by

---

[8] l. 761   In this amorous extravagance,—which reminds us of the conceits of Lovelace, rather than of the Ancients,—it is probably idle to enquire why *Ida* is introduced.

In tranced dulness; speak, and let that spell
Affright this lethargy! I cannot quell
Its heavy pressure, and will press at least   770
My lips to thine, that they may richly feast
Until we taste the life of love again.
What! dost thou move? dost kiss? O bliss! O pain!
I love thee, youth, more than I can conceive;
And so long absence from thee doth bereave   775
My soul of any rest: yet must I hence:
Yet, can I not to starry eminence
Uplift thee; nor for very shame can own
Myself to thee. Ah, dearest, do not groan
Or thou wilt force me from this secrecy,   780
And I must blush in heaven. O that I
Had done it already; that the dreadful smiles
At my lost brightness, my impassion'd wiles,
Had waned from Olympus' solemn height,
And from all serious Gods; that our delight   785
Was quite forgotten, save of us alone!
And wherefore so ashamed? 'Tis but to atone
For endless pleasure, by some coward blushes:
Yet must I be a coward!—Horror rushes
Too palpable before me—the sad look   790
Of Jove—Minerva's start—no bosom shook
With awe of purity—no Cupid pinion
In reverence veiled—my crystaline dominion
Half lost, and all old hymns made nullity!
But what is this to love? O I could fly   795
With thee into the ken of heavenly powers,
So thou wouldst thus, for many sequent hours,
Press me so sweetly. Now I swear at once
That I am wise, that Pallas is a dunce—
Perhaps her love like mine is but unknown—   800
O I do think that I have been alone

In chastity: yes, Pallas has been sighing,
While every eve saw me my hair uptying
With fingers cool as aspen leaves. Sweet love,
I was as vague as solitary dove,   805
Nor knew that nests were built. Now a soft kiss—
Aye, by that kiss, I vow an endless bliss,
An immortality of passion's thine:
Ere long I will exalt thee to the shine
Of heaven ambrosial; and we will shade   810
Ourselves whole summers by a river glade;
And I will tell thee stories of the sky,
And breathe thee whispers of its minstrelsy.
My happy love will overwing all bounds!
O let me melt into thee; let the sounds   815
Of our close voices marry at their birth;
Let us entwine hoveringly—O dearth
Of human words! roughness of mortal speech!
Lispings empyrean will I sometime teach
Thine honied tongue—lute-breathings, which I gasp   820
To have thee understand, now while I clasp
Thee thus, and weep for fondness—I am pain'd,
Endymion: woe! woe! is grief contain'd
In the very deeps of pleasure, my sole life?"—
Hereat, with many sobs, her gentle strife   825
Melted into a languor. He return'd
Entranced vows and tears.

　　　　　　　　　　Ye who have yearn'd
With too much passion, will here stay and pity,
For the mere sake of truth; as 'tis a ditty
Not of these days, but long ago 'twas told   830
By a cavern wind unto a forest old;
And then the forest told it in a dream
To a sleeping lake, whose cool and level gleam

A poet caught as he was journeying
To Phoebus' shrine; and in it he did fling   835
His weary limbs, bathing an hour's space,
And after, straight in that inspired place
He sang the story up into the air,
Giving it universal freedom. There
Has it been ever sounding for those ears   840
Whose tips are glowing hot. The legend cheers
Yon centinel stars; and he who listens to it
Must surely be self-doomed or he will rue it:
For quenchless burnings come upon the heart,
Made fiercer by a fear lest any part   845
Should be engulphed in the eddying wind.
As much as here is penn'd doth always find
A resting place, thus much comes clear and plain;
Anon the strange voice is upon the wane—
And 'tis but echo'd from departing sound,   850
That the fair visitant at last unwound
Her gentle limbs, and left the youth asleep.—
Thus the tradition of the gusty deep.

    Now turn we to our former chroniclers.—
Endymion awoke, that grief of hers   855
Sweet paining on his ear: he sickly guess'd
How lone he was once more, and sadly press'd
His empty arms together, hung his head,
And most forlorn upon that widow'd bed
Sat silently. Love's madness he had known: 860
Often with more than tortured lion's groan
Moanings had burst from him; but now that rage
Had pass'd away: no longer did he wage
A rough-voic'd war against the dooming stars.
No, he had felt too much for such harsh jars: 865
The lyre of his soul Eolian tun'd

Forgot all violence, and but commun'd
With melancholy thought: O he had swoon'd
Drunken from pleasure's nipple; and his love
Henceforth was dove-like.—Loth was he to move   870
From the imprinted couch, and when he did,
'Twas with slow, languid paces, and face hid
In muffling hands. So temper'd, out he stray'd
Half seeing visions that might have dismay'd
Alecto's serpents; ravishments more keen   875
Than Hermes' pipe,[9] when anxious he did lean
Over eclipsing eyes: and at the last
It was a sounding grotto, vaulted, vast,
O'er studded with a thousand, thousand pearls,
And crimson mouthed shells with stubborn curls,   880
Of every shape and size, even to the bulk
In which whales arbour close, to brood and sulk
Against an endless storm. Moreover too,
Fish-semblances, of green and azure hue,
Ready to snort their streams. In this cool wonder   885
Endymion sat down, and 'gan to ponder
On all his life: his youth, up to the day
When 'mid acclaim, and feasts, and garlands gay,
He stept upon his shepherd throne: the look
Of his white palace in wild forest nook,   890
And all the revels he had lorded there:
Each tender maiden whom he once thought fair,
With every friend and fellow-woodlander—
Pass'd like a dream before him. Then the spur
Of the old bards to mighty deeds: his plans   895
To nurse the golden age 'mong shepherd clans:
That wondrous night: the great Pan-festival:

---

[9] l. 876 *Hermes' pipe*: Argus was thus lulled to sleep as he was guarding Io, and slain by Hermes at command of Zeus.

69

His sister's sorrow; and his wanderings all,
Until into the earth's deep maw he rush'd:
Then all its buried magic, till it flush'd   900
High with excessive love. "And now," thought he,
"How long must I remain in jeopardy
Of blank amazements that amaze no more?
Now I have tasted her sweet soul to the core
All other depths are shallow: essences,   905
Once spiritual, are like muddy lees,
Meant but to fertilize my earthly root,
And make my branches lift a golden fruit
Into the bloom of heaven: other light,
Though it be quick and sharp enough to blight   910
The Olympian eagle's vision, is dark,
Dark as the parentage of chaos. Hark!
My silent thoughts are echoing from these shells;
Or they are but the ghosts, the dying swells
Of noises far away?—list!"—Hereupon   915
He kept an anxious ear. The humming tone
Came louder, and behold, there as he lay,
On either side outgush'd, with misty spray,
A copious spring; and both together dash'd
Swift, mad, fantastic round the rocks, and lash'd   920
Among the conchs and shells of the lofty grot,
Leaving a trickling dew. At last they shot
Down from the ceiling's height, pouring a noise
As of some breathless racers whose hopes poize
Upon the last few steps, and with spent force   925
Along the ground they took a winding course.
Endymion follow'd—for it seem'd that one
Ever pursued, the other strove to shun—
Follow'd their languid mazes, till well nigh
He had left thinking of the mystery,—   930
And was now rapt in tender hoverings

70

Over the vanish'd bliss. Ah! what is it sings
His dream away? What melodies are these?
They sound as through the whispering of trees,
Not native in such barren vaults. Give ear!   935

"O Arethusa, peerless nymph! why fear
Such tenderness as mine? Great Dian, why,
Why didst thou hear her prayer? O that I
Were rippling round her dainty fairness now,
Circling about her waist, and striving how   940
To entice her to a dive! then stealing in
Between her luscious lips and eyelids thin.
O that her shining hair was in the sun,
And I distilling from it thence to run
In amorous rillets down her shrinking form!   945
To linger on her lily shoulders, warm
Between her kissing breasts, and every charm
Touch raptur'd!—See how painfully I flow:
Fair maid, be pitiful to my great woe.
Stay, stay thy weary course, and let me lead,   950
A happy wooer, to the flowery mead
Where all that beauty snar'd me."—"Cruel god,
Desist! or my offended mistress' nod
Will stagnate all thy fountains:—tease me not
With syren words—Ah, have I really got   955
Such power to madden thee? And is it true—
Away, away, or I shall dearly rue
My very thoughts: in mercy then away,
Kindest Alpheus for should I obey
My own dear will, 'twould be a deadly bane."—   960
"O, Oread-Queen! would that thou hadst a pain
Like this of mine, then would I fearless turn
And be a criminal."—"Alas, I burn,
I shudder—gentle river, get thee hence.

Alpheus! thou enchanter! every sense   965
Of mine was once made perfect in these woods.
Fresh breezes, bowery lawns, and innocent floods,
Ripe fruits, and lonely couch, contentment gave;
But ever since I heedlessly did lave
In thy deceitful stream, a panting glow   970
Grew strong within me: wherefore serve me so,
And call it love? Alas, 'twas cruelty.
Not once more did I close my happy eyes
Amid the thrush's song. Away! Avaunt!
O 'twas a cruel thing."—"Now thou dost taunt   975
So softly, Arethusa, that I think
If thou wast playing on my shady brink,
Thou wouldst bathe once again. Innocent maid!
Stifle thine heart no more;—nor be afraid
Of angry powers: there are deities   980
Will shade us with their wings. Those fitful sighs
'Tis almost death to hear: O let me pour
A dewy balm upon them!—fear no more,
Sweet Arethusa! Dian's self must feel
Sometimes these very pangs. Dear maiden, steal   985
Blushing into my soul, and let us fly
These dreary caverns for the open sky.
I will delight thee all my winding course,
From the green sea up to my hidden source
About Arcadian forests; and will shew   990
The channels where my coolest waters flow
Through mossy rocks; where, 'mid exuberant green,
I roam in pleasant darkness, more unseen
Than Saturn in his exile; where I brim
Round flowery islands, and take thence a skim   995
Of mealy sweets, which myriads of bees
Buzz from their honied wings: and thou shouldst please
Thyself to choose the richest, where we might

Be incense-pillow'd every summer night.
Doff all sad fears, thou white deliciousness,   1000
And let us be thus comforted; unless
Thou couldst rejoice to see my hopeless stream
Hurry distracted from Sol's temperate beam,
And pour to death along some hungry sands."—
"What can I do, Alpheus? Dian stands   1005
Severe before me: persecuting fate!
Unhappy Arethusa! thou wast late
A huntress free in"—At this, sudden fell
Those two sad streams adown a fearful dell.
The Latmian listen'd, but he heard no more,   1010
Save echo, faint repeating o'er and o'er
The name of Arethusa. On the verge
Of that dark gulph he wept, and said: "I urge
Thee, gentle Goddess of my pilgrimage,
By our eternal hopes, to soothe, to assuage,   1015
If thou art powerful, these lovers pains;
And make them happy in some happy plains.

He turn'd—there was a whelming sound—he stept,
There was a cooler light; and so he kept
Towards it by a sandy path, and lo!   1020
More suddenly than doth a moment go,
The visions of the earth were gone and fled—
He saw the giant sea above his head.

Endymion

BOOK III

THERE are who lord it o'er their fellow-men[1]
With most prevailing tinsel: who unpen
Their baaing vanities, to browse away
The comfortable green and juicy hay
From human pastures; or, O torturing fact!   5
Who, through an idiot blink, will see unpack'd
Fire-branded foxes to sear up and singe
Our gold and ripe-ear'd hopes. With not one tinge
Of sanctuary splendour, not a sight
Able to face an owl's, they still are dight   10
By the blear-eyed nations in empurpled vests,
And crowns, and turbans. With unladen breasts,
Save of blown self-applause, they proudly mount
To their spirit's perch, their being's high account,
Their tiptop nothings, their dull skies, their thrones—   15
Amid the fierce intoxicating tones
Of trumpets, shoutings, and belabour'd drums,
And sudden cannon. Ah! how all this hums,

---

[1] l. 1–20 "It was an unfortunate occurrence," writes Lord Houghton, narrating the introduction of Keats to Leigh Hunt and his associates, "that Keats became unwittingly identified, not only with a literary coterie, with whose specialities he had little in common, but with a supposed political association for revolutionary objects with which he entertained nothing beyond the vaguest sympathy."—In this atmosphere it is no wonder that the Poet's wing should flag, and his verse go heavily. But he soon renews his mighty youth;—nor has the whole poem a lovelier passage, nor one more deeply felt, than the moonlight landscape which concludes the paragraph.

Lines 395–400, on the other hand, are a specimen of the singular prose matter which occasionally occurs, entwined in the golden tissue of the song. This lapse seems to me especially to characterize the transitions, (always so difficult to manage), in the story.

In wakeful ears, like uproar past and gone—
Like thunder clouds that spake to Babylon,   20
And set those old Chaldeans to their tasks.—
Are then regalities all gilded masks?
No, there are throned seats unscalable
But by a patient wing, a constant spell,
Or by ethereal things that, unconfin'd,   25
Can make a ladder of the eternal wind,
And poise about in cloudy thunder-tents
To watch the abysm-birth of elements.
Aye, 'bove the withering of old-lipp'd Fate
A thousand Powers keep religious state,   30
In water, fiery realm, and airy bourne;
And, silent as a consecrated urn,
Hold sphery sessions for a season due.
Yet few of these far majesties, ah, few!
Have bared their operations to this globe—   35
Few, who with gorgeous pageantry enrobe
Our piece of heaven—whose benevolence
Shakes hand with our own Ceres; every sense
Filling with spiritual sweets to plenitude,
As bees gorge full their cells. And, by the feud   40
'Twixt Nothing and Creation, I here swear,
Eterne Apollo! that thy Sister fair
Is of all these the gentlier-mightiest.
When thy gold breath is misting in the west,
She unobserved steals unto her throne,   45
And there she sits most meek and most alone;
As if she had not pomp subservient;
As if thine eye, high Poet! was not bent
Towards her with the Muses in thine heart;
As if the ministring stars kept not apart,   50
Waiting for silver-footed messages.
O Moon! the oldest shades 'mong oldest trees

Feel palpitations when thou lookest in:
O Moon! old boughs lisp forth a holier din
The while they feel thine airy fellowship.   55
Thou dost bless every where, with silver lip
Kissing dead things to life. The sleeping kine,
Couched in thy brightness, dream of fields divine:
Innumerable mountains rise, and rise,
Ambitious for the hallowing of thine eyes;   60
And yet thy benediction passeth not
One obscure hiding-place, one little spot
Where pleasure may be sent: the nested wren
Has thy fair face within its tranquil ken,
And from beneath a sheltering ivy leaf   65
Takes glimpses of thee; thou art a relief
To the poor patient oyster, where it sleeps
Within its pearly house.—The mighty deeps,
The monstrous sea is thine—the myriad sea!
O Moon! far-spooming Ocean bows to thee,   70
And Tellus feels his forehead's cumbrous load.

   Cynthia! where art thou now? What far abode
Of green or silvery bower doth enshrine
Such utmost beauty? Alas, thou dost pine
For one as sorrowful: thy cheek is pale   75
For one whose cheek is pale: thou dost bewail
His tears, who weeps for thee. Where dost thou sigh?
Ah! surely that light peeps from Vesper's eye,
Or what a thing is love! 'Tis She, but lo!
How chang'd, how full of ache, how gone in woe!   80
She dies at the thinnest cloud; her loveliness
Is wan on Neptune's blue: yet there's a stress
Of love-spangles, just off yon cape of trees,
Dancing upon the waves, as if to please
The curly foam with amorous influence.   85

O, not so idle: for down-glancing thence
She fathoms eddies, and runs wild about
O'erwhelming water-courses; scaring out
The thorny sharks from hiding-holes, and fright'ning
Their savage eyes with unaccustomed lightning.   90
Where will the splendor be content to reach?
O love! how potent hast thou been to teach
Strange journeyings! Wherever beauty dwells,
In gulf or aerie, mountains or deep dells,
In light, in gloom, in star or blazing sun,   95
Thou pointest out the way, and straight 'tis won.
Amid his toil thou gav'st Leander breath;
Thou leddest Orpheus through the gleams of death;
Thou madest Pluto bear thin element;
And now, O winged Chieftain! thou hast sent   100
A moon-beam to the deep, deep water-world,
To find Endymion.

On gold sand impearl'd
With lily shells, and pebbles milky white,
Poor Cynthia greeted him, and sooth'd her light
Against his pallid face: he felt the charm   105
To breathlessness, and suddenly a warm
Of his heart's blood: 'twas very sweet; he stay'd
His wandering steps, and half-entranced laid
His head upon a tuft of straggling weeds,
To taste the gentle moon, and freshening beads,   110
Lashed from the crystal roof by fishes' tails.
And so he kept, until the rosy veils
Mantling the east, by Aurora's peering hand
Were lifted from the water's breast, and fann'd
Into sweet air; and sober'd morning came   115
Meekly through billows:—when like taper-flame
Left sudden by a dallying breath of air,

He rose in silence, and once more 'gan fare
Along his fated way.

Far had he roam'd,[2]
With nothing save the hollow vast, that foam'd   120
Above, around, and at his feet; save things
More dead than Morpheus' imaginings:
Old rusted anchors, helmets, breast-plates large
Of gone sea-warriors; brazen beaks and targe;
Rudders that for a hundred years had lost   125
The sway of human hand; gold vase emboss'd
With long-forgotten story, and wherein
No reveller had ever dipp'd a chin
But those of Saturn's vintage; mouldering scrolls,
Writ in the tongue of heaven, by those souls   130
Who first were on the earth; and sculptures rude
In ponderous stone, developing the mood
Of ancient Nox;—then skeletons of man,
Of beast, behemoth, and leviathan,
And elephant, and eagle, and huge jaw   135
Of nameless monster. A cold leaden awe
These secrets struck into him; and unless
Dian had chaced away that heaviness,
He might have died: but now, with cheered feel,
He onward kept; wooing these thoughts to steal   140
About the labyrinth in his soul of love.

"What is there in thee, Moon! that thou shouldst move
My heart so potently? When yet a child
I oft have dried my tears when thou hast smil'd.

---

[2] l. 119-136 Two other magnificent pictures of the world beneath sea may be compared with this: Clarence's dream in *Richard III,* and the vision related by Panthea in *Prometheuus Unbound,* Act iv.—Keats, at twenty-two, fairly rises to his place beside Shakespeare and Shelley.

Thou seem'dst my sister: hand in hand we went   145
From eve to morn across the firmament.
No apples would I gather from the tree,
Till thou hadst cool'd their cheeks deliciously:
No tumbling water ever spake romance,
But when my eyes with thine thereon could dance: 150
No woods were green enough, no bower divine,
Until thou liftedst up thine eyelids fine:
In sowing time ne'er would I dibble take,
Or drop a seed, till thou wast wide awake;
And, in the summer tide of blossoming,   155
No one but thee hath heard me blithly sing
And mesh my dewy flowers all the night.
No melody was like a passing spright
If it went not to solemnize thy reign.
Yes, in my boyhood, every joy and pain   160
By thee were fashion'd to the self-same end;
And as I grew in years, still didst thou blend
With all my ardours: thou wast the deep glen;
Thou wast the mountain-top—the sage's pen—
The poet's harp—the voice of friends—the sun;   165
Thou wast the river—thou wast glory won;
Thou wast my clarion's blast—thou wast my steed—
My goblet full of wine—my topmost deed:—
Thou wast the charm of women, lovely Moon!
O what a wild and harmonized tune   170
My spirit struck from all the beautiful!
On some bright essence could I lean, and lull
Myself to immortality: I prest
Nature's soft pillow in a wakeful rest.
But, gentle Orb! there came a nearer bliss—   175
My strange love came—Felicity's abyss!
She came, and thou didst fade, and fade away—
Yet not entirely; no, thy starry sway

Has been an under-passion to this hour.
Now I begin to feel thine orby power   180
Is coming fresh upon me: O be kind,
Keep back thine influence, and do not blind
My sovereign vision.—Dearest love, forgive
That I can think away from thee and live!—
Pardon me, airy planet, that I prize   185
One thought beyond thine argent luxuries!
How far beyond!" At this a surpris'd start
Frosted the springing verdure of his heart;
For as he lifted up his eyes to swear
How his own goddess was past all things fair,   190
He saw far in the concave green of the sea
An old man sitting calm and peacefully.
Upon a weeded rock this old man sat,
And his white hair was awful, and a mat
Of weeds were cold beneath his cold thin feet;   195
And, ample as the largest winding-sheet,
A cloak of blue wrapp'd up his aged bones,
O'erwrought with symbols by the deepest groans
Of ambitious magic: every ocean-form
Was woven in with black distinctness; storm,   200
And calm, and whispering, and hideous roar
Were emblem'd in the woof; with every shape
That skims, or dives, or sleeps, 'twixt cape and cape.
The gulphing whale was like a dot in the spell,
Yet look upon it, and 'twould size and swell   205
To its huge self; and the minutest fish
Would pass the very hardest gazer's wish,
And show his little eye's anatomy.
Then there was pictur'd the regality
Of Neptune; and the sea nymphs round his state,   210
In beauteous vassalage, look up and wait.
Beside this old man lay a pearly wand,

And in his lap a book, the which he conn'd
So stedfastly, that the new denizen
Had time to keep him in amazed ken,   215
To mark these shadowings, and stand in awe.

   The old man rais'd his hoary head and saw
The wilder'd stranger—seeming not to see,
His features were so lifeless. Suddenly
He woke as from a trance; his snow-white brows   220
Went arching up, and like two magic ploughs
Furrow'd deep wrinkles in his forehead large,
Which kept as fixedly as rocky marge,
Till round his wither'd lips had gone a smile.
Then up he rose, like one whose tedious toil   225
Had watch'd for years in forlorn hermitage,
Who had not from mid-life to utmost age
Eas'd in one accent his o'er-burden'd soul,
Even to the trees. He rose: he grasp'd his stole,
With convuls'd clenches waving it abroad,   230
And in a voice of solemn joy, that aw'd
Echo into oblivion, he said:—

   "Thou art the man! Now shall I lay my head
In peace upon my watery pillow: now
Sleep will come smoothly to my weary brow.   235
O Jove! I shall be young again, be young!
O shell-borne Neptune, I am pierc'd and stung
With new-born life! What shall I do? Where go,
When I have cast this serpent-skin of woe?—
I'll swim to the syrens, and one moment listen   240
Their melodies, and see their long hair glisten;
Anon upon that giant's arm I'll be,
That writhes about the roots of Sicily:
To northern seas I'll in a twinkling sail,

And mount upon the snortings of a whale 245
To some black cloud; thence down I'll madly sweep
On forked lightning, to the deepest deep,
Where through some sucking pool I will be hurl'd
With rapture to the other side of the world!
O, I am full of gladness! Sisters three, 250
I bow full hearted to your old decree!
Yes, every god be thank'd, and power benign,
For I no more shall wither, droop, and pine.
Thou art the man!" Endymion started back
Dismay'd; and, like a wretch from whom the rack 255
Tortures hot breath, and speech of agony,
Mutter'd: "What lonely death am I to die
In this cold region? Will he let me freeze,
And float my brittle limbs o'er polar seas?
Or will he touch me with his searing hand, 260
And leave a black memorial on the sand?
Or tear me piece-meal with a bony saw,
And keep me as a chosen food to draw
His magian fish through hated fire and flame?
O misery of hell! resistless, tame, 265
Am I to be burnt up? No, I will shout,
Until the gods through heaven's blue look out!—
O Tartarus! but some few days agone
Her soft arms were entwining me, and on
Her voice I hung like fruit among green leaves: 270
Her lips were all my own, and—ah, ripe sheaves
Of happiness! ye on the stubble droop,
But never may be garner'd. I must stoop
My head, and kiss death's foot. Love! love, farewel!
Is there no hope from thee? This horrid spell 275
Would melt at thy sweet breath.—By Dian's hind
Feeding from her white fingers, on the wind

I see thy streaming hair! and now, by Pan,
I care not for this old mysterious man!"

He spake, and walking to that aged form,   280
Look'd high defiance. Lo! his heart 'gan warm
With pity, for the grey-hair'd creature wept.
Had he then wrong'd a heart where sorrow kept?
Had he, though blindly contumelious, brought
Rheum to kind eyes, a sting to human thought,   285
Convulsion to a mouth of many years?
He had in truth; and he was ripe for tears.
The penitent shower fell, as down he knelt
Before that care-worn sage, who trembling felt
About his large dark locks, and faultering spake: 290

"Arise, good youth, for sacred Phoebus' sake!
I know thine inmost bosom, and I feel
A very brother's yearning for thee steal
Into mine own: for why? thou openest
The prison gates that have so long opprest   295
My weary watching. Though thou know'st it not,
Thou art commission'd to this fated spot
For great enfranchisement. O weep no more;
I am a friend to love, to loves of yore:
Aye, hadst thou never lov'd an unknown power   300
I had been grieving at this joyous hour
But even now most miserable old,
I saw thee, and my blood no longer cold
Gave mighty pulses: in this tottering case
Grew a new heart, which at this moment plays   305
As dancingly as thine. Be not afraid,
For thou shalt hear this secret all display'd,
Now as we speed towards our joyous task."

So saying, this young soul in age's mask
Went forward with the Carian side by side: 310
Resuming quickly thus; while ocean's tide
Hung swollen at their backs, and jewel'd sands
Took silently their foot-prints.

                              "My soul stands
Now past the midway from mortality,
And so I can prepare without a sigh   315
To tell thee briefly all my joy and pain.
I was a fisher once, upon this main,
And my boat danc'd in every creek and bay;
Rough billows were my home by night and day,—
The sea-gulls not more constant; for I had   320
No housing from the storm and tempests mad,
But hollow rocks,—and they were palaces
Of silent happiness, of slumberous ease:
Long years of misery have told me so.
Aye, thus it was one thousand years ago.   325
One thousand years!—Is it then possible
To look so plainly through them? to dispel
A thousand years with backward glance sublime?
To breathe away as 'twere all scummy slime
From off a crystal pool, to see its deep,   330
And one's own image from the bottom peep?
Yes: now I am no longer wretched thrall,
My long captivity and moanings all
Are but a slime, a thin-pervading scum,
The which I breathe away, and thronging come   335
Like things of yesterday my youthful pleasures.

     "I touch'd no lute, I sang not, trod no measures:
I was a lonely youth on desert shores.
My sports were lonely, 'mid continuous roars,

And craggy isles, and sea-mew's plaintive cry   340
Plaining discrepant between sea and sky.
Dolphins were still my playmates; shapes unseen
Would let me feel their scales of gold and green,
Nor be my desolation; and, full oft,
When a dread waterspout had rear'd aloft   345
Its hungry hugeness, seeming ready ripe
To burst with hoarsest thunderings, and wipe
My life away like a vast sponge of fate,
Some friendly monster, pitying my sad state,
Has dived to its foundations, gulph'd it down,   350
And left me tossing safely. But the crown
Of all my life was utmost quietude:
More did I love to lie in cavern rude,
Keeping in wait whole days for Neptune's voice,
And if it came at last, hark, and rejoice!   355
There blush'd no summer eve but I would steer
My skiff along green shelving coasts, to hear
The shepherd's pipe come clear from aery steep,
Mingled with ceaseless bleatings of his sheep:
And never was a day of summer shine,   360
But I beheld its birth upon the brine:
For I would watch all night to see unfold
Heaven's gates, and Aethon snort his morning gold
Wide o'er the swelling streams: and constantly
At brim of day-tide, on some grassy lea,   365
My nets would be spread out, and I at rest.
The poor folk of the sea-country I blest
With daily boon of fish most delicate:
They knew not whence this bounty, and elate
Would strew sweet flowers on a sterile beach.   370

"Why was I not contented? Wherefore reach
At things which, but for thee, O Latmian!

Had been my dreary death? Fool! I began
To feel distemper'd longings: to desire
The utmost privilege that ocean's sire   375
Could grant in benediction: to be free
Of all his kingdom. Long in misery
I wasted, ere in one extremest fit
I plung'd for life or death. To interknit
One's senses with so dense a breathing stuff   380
Might seem a work of pain; so not enough
Can I admire how crystal-smooth it felt,
And buoyant round my limbs. At first I dwelt
Whole days and days in sheer astonishment;
Forgetful utterly of self-intent;   385
Moving but with the mighty ebb and flow.
Then, like a new fledg'd bird that first doth shew
His spreaded feathers to the morrow chill,
I tried in fear the pinions of my will.
'Twas freedom! and at once I visited   390
The ceaseless wonders of this ocean-bed.
No need to tell thee of them, for I see
That thou hast been a witness—it must be
For these I know thou canst not feel a drouth,
By the melancholy corners of that mouth.   395
So I will in my story straightway pass
To more immediate matter. Woe, alas!
That love should be my bane! Ah, Scylla fair!
Why did poor Glaucus ever—ever dare
To sue thee to his heart? Kind stranger-youth!   400
I lov'd her to the very white of truth,
And she would not conceive it. Timid thing!
She fled me swift as sea-bird on the wing,
Round every isle, and point, and promontory,

From where large Hercules[3] wound up his story   405
Far as Egyptian Nile. My passion grew
The more, the more I saw her dainty hue
Gleam delicately through the azure clear:
Until 'twas too fierce agony to bear;
And in that agony, across my grief   410
It flash'd, that Circe might find some relief—
Cruel enchantress! So above the water
I rear'd my head, and look'd for Phoebus' daughter.
Aeaea's isle was wondering at the moon:—
It seem'd to whirl around me, and a swoon   415
Left me dead-drifting to that fatal power.

"When I awoke, 'twas in a twilight bower;
Just when the light of morn, with hum of bees,
Stole through its verdurous matting of fresh trees.
How sweet, and sweeter! for I heard a lyre,   420
And over it a sighing voice expire.
It ceased—I caught light footsteps; and anon
The fairest face that morn e'er look'd upon
Push'd through a screen of roses. Starry Jove!
With tears, and smiles, and honey-words she wove   425
A net whose thraldom was more bliss than all
The range of flower'd Elysium. Thus did fall
The dew of her rich speech: "Ah! Art awake?
O let me hear thee speak, for Cupid's sake!
I am so oppress'd with joy! Why, I have shed   430
An urn of tears, as though thou wert cold dead;
And now I find thee living, I will pour
From these devoted eyes their silver store,
Until exhausted of the latest drop,
So it will pleasure thee, and force thee stop   435

---

[3] l. 405 *Hercules:* From Gades to Egypt.

Here, that I too may live: but if beyond
Such cool and sorrowful offerings, thou art fond
Of soothing warmth, of dalliance supreme;
If thou art ripe to taste a long love dream;
If smiles, if dimples, tongues for ardour mute,   440
Hang in thy vision like a tempting fruit,
O let me pluck it for thee." Thus she link'd
Her charming syllables, till indistinct
Their music came to my o'er-sweeten'd soul;
And then she hover'd over me, and stole   445
So near, that if no nearer it had been
This furrow'd visage thou hadst never seen.

"Young man of Latmos! thus particular
Am I, that thou may'st plainly see how far
This fierce temptation went: and thou may'st not   450
Exclaim, How then, was Scylla quite forgot?

"Who could resist? Who in this universe?
She did so breathe ambrosia; so immerse
My fine existence in a golden clime.
She took me like a child of suckling time,   455
And cradled me in roses. Thus condemn'd,
The current of my former life was stemm'd,
And to this arbitrary queen of sense
I bow'd a tranced vassal: nor would thence
Have mov'd, even though Amphion's harp had woo'd   460
Me back to Scylla o'er the billows rude.
For as Apollo each eve doth devise
A new appareling for western skies;
So every eve, nay every spendthrift hour
Shed balmy consciousness within that bower.   465
And I was free of haunts umbrageous;
Could wander in the mazy forest-house

88

Of squirrels, foxes shy, and antler'd deer,
And birds from coverts innermost and drear
Warbling for very joy mellifluous sorrow—   470
To me new born delights!

                "Now let me borrow,
For moments few, a temperament as stern
As Pluto's sceptre, that my words not burn
These uttering lips, while I in calm speech tell
How specious heaven was changed to real hell.   475

    "One morn she left me sleeping: half awake
I sought for her smooth arms and lips, to slake
My greedy thirst with nectarous camel-draughts;
But she was gone. Whereat the barbed shafts
Of disappointment stuck in me so sore,   480
That out I ran and search'd the forest o'er.
Wandering about in pine and cedar gloom
Damp awe assail'd me; for there 'gan to boom
A sound of moan, an agony of sound,
Sepulchral from the distance all around.   485
Then came a conquering earth-thunder, and rumbled
That fierce complain to silence: while I stumbled
Down a precipitous path, as if impell'd.
I came to a dark valley.—Groanings swell'd
Poisonous about my ears, and louder grew,   490
The nearer I approach'd a flame's gaunt blue,
That glar'd before me through a thorny brake.
This fire, like the eye of gordian snake,
Bewitch'd me towards; and I soon was near
A sight too fearful for the feel of fear: 495
In thicket hid I curs'd the haggard scene—
The banquet of my arms, my arbour queen,
Seated upon an uptorn forest root;

And all around her shapes, wizard and brute,
Laughing, and wailing, groveling, serpenting,   500
Shewing tooth, tusk, and venom-bag, and sting!
O such deformities! Old Charon's self,
Should he give up awhile his penny pelf,
And take a dream 'mong rushes Stygian,
It could not be so phantasied. Fierce, wan,   505
And tyrannizing was the lady's look,
As over them a gnarled staff she shook.
Oft-times upon the sudden she laugh'd out,
And from a basket emptied to the rout
Clusters of grapes, the which they raven'd quick   510
And roar'd for more; with many a hungry lick
About their shaggy jaws. Avenging, slow,
Anon she took a branch of mistletoe,
And emptied on't a black dull-gurgling phial:
Groan'd one and all, as if some piercing trial   515
Was sharpening for their pitiable bones.
She lifted up the charm: appealing groans
From their poor breasts went sueing to her ear
In vain; remorseless as an infant's bier
She whisk'd against their eyes the sooty oil.   520
Whereat was heard a noise of painful toil,
Increasing gradual to a tempest rage,
Shrieks, yells, and groans of torture-pilgrimage;
Until their grieved bodies 'gan to bloat
And puff from the tail's end to stifled throat: 525
Then was appalling silence: then a sight
More wildering than all that hoarse affright;
For the whole herd, as by a whirlwind writhen,
Went through the dismal air like one huge Python
Antagonizing Boreas,—and so vanish'd.   530
Yet there was not a breath of wind: she banish'd
These phantoms with a nod. Lo! from the dark

Came waggish fauns, and nymphs, and satyrs stark,
With dancing and loud revelry,—and went
Swifter than centaurs after rapine bent.—   535
Sighing an elephant appear'd and bow'd
Before the fierce witch, speaking thus aloud
In human accent: "Potent goddess! chief
Of pains resistless! make my being brief,
Or let me from this heavy prison fly: 540
Or give me to the air, or let me die!
I sue not for my happy crown again;
I sue not for my phalanx on the plain;
I sue not for my lone, my widow'd wife;
I sue not for my ruddy drops of life,   545
My children fair, my lovely girls and boys!
I will forget them; I will pass these joys;
Ask nought so heavenward, so too—too high:
Only I pray, as fairest boon, to die,
Or be deliver'd from this cumbrous flesh,   550
From this gross, detestable, filthy mesh,
And merely given to the cold bleak air.
Have mercy, Goddess! Circe, feel my prayer!"

    That curst magician's name fell icy numb
Upon my wild conjecturing: truth had come   555
Naked and sabre-like against my heart.
I saw a fury whetting a death-dart;
And my slain spirit, overwrought with fright,
Fainted away in that dark lair of night.
Think, my deliverer, how desolate   560
My waking must have been! disgust, and hate,
And terrors manifold divided me
A spoil amongst them. I prepar'd to flee
Into the dungeon core of that wild wood:
I fled three days—when lo! before me stood   565

91

Glaring the angry witch. O Dis, even now,
A clammy dew is beading on my brow,
At mere remembering her pale laugh, and curse.
"Ha! ha! Sir Dainty! there must be a nurse
Made of rose leaves and thistledown, express,   570
To cradle thee my sweet, and lull thee: yes,
I am too flinty-hard for thy nice touch:
My tenderest squeeze is but a giant's clutch.
So, fairy-thing, it shall have lullabies
Unheard of yet; and it shall still its cries   575
Upon some breast more lily-feminine.
Oh, no—it shall not pine, and pine, and pine
More than one pretty, trifling thousand years;
And then 'twere pity, but fate's gentle shears
Cut short its immortality. Sea-flirt!   580
Young dove of the waters! truly I'll not hurt
One hair of thine: see how I weep and sigh,
That our heart-broken parting is so nigh.
And must we part? Ah, yes, it must be so.
Yet ere thou leavest me in utter woe,   585
Let me sob over thee my last adieus,
And speak a blessing: Mark me! thou hast thews
Immortal, for thou art of heavenly race:
But such a love is mine, that here I chase
Eternally away from thee all bloom   590
Of youth, and destine thee towards a tomb.
Hence shalt thou quickly to the watery vast;
And there, ere many days be overpast,
Disabled age shall seize thee; and even then
Thou shalt not go the way of aged men;   595
But live and wither, cripple and still breathe
Ten hundred years: which gone, I then bequeath
Thy fragile bones to unknown burial.
Adieu, sweet love, adieu!"—As shot stars fall,

She fled ere I could groan for mercy. Stung   600
And poisoned was my spirit: despair sung
A war-song of defiance 'gainst all hell.
A hand was at my shoulder to compel
My sullen steps; another 'fore my eyes
Moved on with pointed finger. In this guise   605
Enforced, at the last by ocean's foam
I found me; by my fresh, my native home.
Its tempering coolness, to my life akin,
Came salutary as I waded in;
And, with a blind voluptuous rage, I gave   610
Battle to the swollen billow-ridge, and drave
Large froth before me, while there yet remain'd
Hale strength, nor from my bones all marrow drain'd.

"Young lover, I must weep—such hellish spite
With dry cheek who can tell? While thus my might   615
Proving upon this element, dismay'd,
Upon a dead thing's face my hand I laid;
I look'd—'twas Scylla! Cursed, cursed Circe!
O vulture-witch, hast never heard of mercy?
Could not thy harshest vengeance be content,   620
But thou must nip this tender innocent
Because I lov'd her?—Cold, O cold indeed
Were her fair limbs, and like a common weed
The sea-swell took her hair. Dead as she was
I clung about her waist, nor ceas'd to pass   625
Fleet as an arrow through unfathom'd brine,
Until there shone a fabric crystalline,
Ribb'd and inlaid with coral, pebble, and pearl.
Headlong I darted; at one eager swirl
Gain'd its bright portal, enter'd, and behold!   630
'Twas vast, and desolate, and icy-cold;
And all around—But wherefore this to thee

Who in few minutes more thyself shalt see?—
I left poor Scylla in a niche and fled.
My fever'd parchings up, my scathing dread   635
Met palsy half way: soon these limbs became
Gaunt, wither'd, sapless, feeble, cramp'd, and lame.

"Now let me pass a cruel, cruel space,
Without one hope, without one faintest trace
Of mitigation, or redeeming bubble   640
Of colour'd phantasy; for I fear 'twould trouble
Thy brain to loss of reason: and next tell
How a restoring chance came down to quell
One half of the witch in me.

                              "On a day,
Sitting upon a rock above the spray,   645
I saw grow up from the horizon's brink
A gallant vessel: soon she seem'd to sink
Away from me again, as though her course
Had been resum'd in spite of hindering force—
So vanish'd: and not long, before arose   650
Dark clouds, and muttering of winds morose.
Old Eolus would stifle his mad spleen,
But could not: therefore all the billows green
Toss'd up the silver spume against the clouds.
The tempest came: I saw that vessel's shrouds   655
In perilous bustle; while upon the deck
Stood trembling creatures. I beheld the wreck;
The final gulphing; the poor struggling souls:
I heard their cries amid loud thunder-rolls.
O they had all been sav'd but crazed eld   660
Annull'd my vigorous cravings: and thus quell'd
And curb'd, think on't, O Latmian! did I sit
Writhing with pity, and a cursing fit

Against that hell-born Circe. The crew had gone,
By one and one, to pale oblivion;   665
And I was gazing on the surges prone,
With many a scalding tear and many a groan,
When at my feet emerg'd an old man's hand,
Grasping this scroll, and this same slender wand.
I knelt with pain—reached out my hand—had grasp'd   670
These treasures—touch'd the knuckles—they unclasp'd—
I caught a finger: but the downward weight
O'erpowered me—it sank. Then 'gan abate
The storm, and through chill aguish gloom outburst
The comfortable sun. I was athirst   675
To search the book, and in the warming air
Parted its dripping leaves with eager care.
Strange matters did it treat of, and drew on
My soul page after page, till well-nigh won
Into forgetfulness; when, stupefied,   680
I read these words, and read again, and tried
My eyes against the heavens, and read again.
O what a load of misery and pain
Each Atlas-line bore off!—a shine of hope
Came gold around me, cheering me to cope   685
Strenuous with hellish tyranny. Attend!
For thou hast brought their promise to an end.

"In the wide sea there lives a forlorn wretch,
Doom'd with enfeebled carcase to outstretch
His loath'd existence through ten centuries,   690
And then to die alone. Who can devise
A total opposition? No one. So
One million times ocean must ebb and flow,
And he oppressed. Yet he shall not die,
These things accomplish'd:—If he utterly   695
Scans all the depths of magic, and expounds

The meanings of all motions, shapes, and sounds;
If he explores all forms and substances
Straight homeward to their symbol-essences;
He shall not die. Moreover, and in chief,   700
He must pursue this task of joy and grief
Most piously;—all lovers tempest-tost,
And in the savage overwhelming lost,
He shall deposit side by side, until
Time's creeping shall the dreary space fulfil: 705
Which done, and all these labours ripened,
A youth, by heavenly power lov'd and led,
Shall stand before him; whom he shall direct
How to consummate all. The youth elect
Must do the thing, or both will be destroy'd."—   710

 "Then," cried the young Endymion, overjoy'd,
"We are twin brothers in this destiny!
Say, I intreat thee, what achievement high
Is, in this restless world, for me reserv'd.
What! if from thee my wandering feet had swerv'd,   715
Had we both perish'd?"—"Look!" the sage replied,
"Dost thou not mark a gleaming through the tide,
Of divers brilliances? 'tis the edifice
I told thee of, where lovely Scylla lies;
And where I have enshrined piously   720
All lovers, whom fell storms have doom'd to die
Throughout my bondage." Thus discoursing, on
They went till unobscur'd the porches shone;
Which hurryingly they gain'd, and enter'd straight.
Sure never since king Neptune held his state   725
Was seen such wonder underneath the stars.
Turn to some level plain where haughty Mars
Has legion'd all his battle; and behold
How every soldier, with firm foot, doth hold

His even breast: see, many steeled squares,   730
And rigid ranks of iron—whence who dares
One step? Imagine further, line by line,
These warrior thousands on the field supine:—
So in that crystal place, in silent rows,
Poor lovers lay at rest from joys and woes.—   735
The stranger from the mountains, breathless, trac'd
Such thousands of shut eyes in order plac'd;
Such ranges of white feet, and patient lips
All ruddy,—for here death no blossom nips.
He mark'd their brows and foreheads; saw their hair   740
Put sleekly on one side with nicest care;
And each one's gentle wrists, with reverence,
Put cross-wise to its heart.

                              "Let us commence,
Whisper'd the guide, stuttering with joy, even now."
He spake, and, trembling like an aspen-bough,   745
Began to tear his scroll in pieces small,
Uttering the while some mumblings funeral.
He tore it into pieces small as snow
That drifts unfeather'd when bleak northerns blow;
And having done it, took his dark blue cloak   750
And bound it round Endymion: then struck
His wand against the empty air times nine.—
"What more there is to do, young man, is thine:
But first a little patience; first undo
This tangled thread, and wind it to a clue.   755
Ah, gentle! 'tis as weak as spider's skein;
And shouldst thou break it—What, is it done so clean?
A power overshadows thee! Oh, brave!
The spite of hell is tumbling to its grave.
Here is a shell; 'tis pearly blank to me,   760
Nor mark'd with any sign or charactery—

Canst thou read aught? O read for pity's sake!
Olympus! we are safe! Now, Carian, break
This wand against yon lyre on the pedestal."

'Twas done: and straight with sudden swell and fall   765
Sweet music breath'd her soul away, and sigh'd
A lullaby to silence.—"Youth! now strew
These minced leaves on me, and passing through
Those files of dead, scatter the same around,
And thou wilt see the issue."—'Mid the sound   770
Of flutes and viols, ravishing his heart,
Endymion from Glaucus stood apart,
And scatter'd in his face some fragments light.
How lightning-swift the change! a youthful wight
Smiling beneath a coral diadem,   775
Out-sparkling sudden like an upturn'd gem,
Appear'd, and, stepping to a beauteous corse,
Kneel'd down beside it, and with tenderest force
Press'd its cold hand, and wept—and Scylla sigh'd!
Endymion, with quick hand, the charm applied—   780
The nymph arose: he left them to their joy,
And onward went upon his high employ,
Showering those powerful fragments on the dead.
And, as he pass'd, each lifted up its head,
As doth a flower at Apollo's touch.   785
Death felt it to his inwards; 'twas too much:
Death fell a weeping in his charnel-house.
The Latmian persever'd along, and thus
All were re-animated. There arose
A noise of harmony, pulses and throes   790
Of gladness in the air—while many, who
Had died in mutual arms devout and true,
Sprang to each other madly; and the rest
Felt a high certainty of being blest.

They gaz'd upon Endymion. Enchantment 795
Grew drunken, and would have its head and bent.
Delicious symphonies, like airy flowers,
Budded, and swell'd, and, full-blown, shed full showers
Of light, soft, unseen leaves of sounds divine.
The two deliverers tasted a pure wine 800
Of happiness, from fairy-press ooz'd out.
Speechless they eyed each other, and about
The fair assembly wander'd to and fro,
Distracted with the richest overflow
Of joy that ever pour'd from heaven.

⸻"Away!" 805
Shouted the new-born god; "Follow, and pay
Our piety to Neptunus supreme!"—
Then Scylla, blushing sweetly from her dream,
They led on first, bent to her meek surprise,
Through portal columns of a giant size, 810
Into the vaulted, boundless emerald.
Joyous all follow'd, as the leader call'd,
Down marble steps; pouring as easily
As hour-glass sand—and fast, as you might see
Swallows obeying the south summer's call, 815
Or swans upon a gentle waterfall.

Thus went that beautiful multitude, nor far,
Ere from among some rocks of glittering spar,
Just within ken, they saw descending thick
Another multitude. Whereat more quick 820
Moved either host. On a wide sand they met,
And of those numbers every eye was wet;
For each their old love found. A murmuring rose,
Like what was never heard in all the throes

Of wind and waters: 'tis past human wit   825
To tell; 'tis dizziness to think of it.

    This mighty consummation made, the host
Mov'd on for many a league; and gain'd, and lost
Huge sea-marks; vanward swelling in array,
And from the rear diminishing away,—   830
Till a faint dawn surpris'd them. Glaucus cried,
"Behold! behold, the palace of his pride!
God Neptune's palaces!" With noise increas'd,
They shoulder'd on towards that brightening east.
At every onward step proud domes arose   835
In prospect,—diamond gleams, and golden glows
Of amber 'gainst their faces levelling.
Joyous, and many as the leaves in spring,
Still onward; still the splendour gradual swell'd.
Rich opal domes were seen, on high upheld   840
By jasper pillars, letting through their shafts
A blush of coral. Copious wonder-draughts
Each gazer drank; and deeper drank more near:
For what poor mortals fragment up, as mere
As marble was there lavish, to the vast   845
Of one fair palace, that far far surpass'd,
Even for common bulk, those olden three,
Memphis, and Babylon, and Nineveh.

    As large, as bright, as colour'd as the bow
Of Iris, when unfading it doth shew   850
Beyond a silvery shower, was the arch
Through which this Paphian army took its march,
Into the outer courts of Neptune's state:
Whence could be seen, direct, a golden gate,
To which the leaders sped; but not half raught   855
Ere it burst open swift as fairy thought,

And made those dazzled thousands veil their eyes
Like callow eagles at the first sunrise.
Soon with an eagle nativeness their gaze
Ripe from hue-golden swoons took all the blaze,   860
And then, behold! large Neptune on his throne
Of emerald deep: yet not exalt alone;
At his right hand stood winged Love, and on
His left sat smiling Beauty's paragon.

    Far as the mariner on highest mast   865
Can see all round upon the calmed vast,
So wide was Neptune's hall: and as the blue
Doth vault the waters, so the waters drew
Their doming curtains, high, magnificent,
Aw'd from the throne aloof;—and when storm-rent   870
Disclos'd the thunder-gloomings in Jove's air;
But sooth'd as now, flash'd sudden everywhere,
Noiseless, sub-marine cloudlets, glittering
Death to a human eye: for there did spring
From natural west, and east, and south, and north,   875
A light as of four sunsets, blazing forth
A gold-green zenith 'bove the Sea-God's head.
Of lucid depth the floor, and far outspread
As breezeless lake, on which the slim canoe
Of feather'd Indian darts about, as through   880
The delicatest air: air verily,
But for the portraiture of clouds and sky:
This palace floor breath-air,—but for the amaze
Of deep-seen wonders motionless,—and blaze
Of the dome pomp, reflected in extremes,   885
Globing a golden sphere.

                  They stood in dreams
Till Triton blew his horn. The palace rang;

The Nereids danc'd; the Syrens faintly sang;
And the great Sea-King bow'd his dripping head.
Then Love took wing, and from his pinions shed   890
On all the multitude a nectarous dew.
The ooze-born Goddess beckoned and drew
Fair Scylla and her guides to conference;
And when they reach'd the throned eminence
She kist the sea-nymph's cheek,—who sat her down   895
A toying with the doves. Then,—"Mighty crown
And sceptre of this kingdom!" Venus said,
"Thy vows were on a time to Nais paid:
Behold!"—Two copious tear-drops instant fell
From the God's large eyes; he smil'd delectable,   900
And over Glaucus held his blessing hands.—
"Endymion! Ah! still wandering in the bands
Of love? Now this is cruel. Since the hour
I met thee in earth's bosom, all my power
Have I put forth to serve thee. What, not yet   905
Escap'd from dull mortality's harsh net?
A little patience, youth! 'twill not be long,
Or I am skilless quite: an idle tongue,
A humid eye, and steps luxurious,
Where these are new and strange, are ominous.   910
Aye, I have seen these signs in one of heaven,
When others were all blind; and were I given
To utter secrets, haply I might say
Some pleasant words:—but Love will have his day.
So wait awhile expectant. Pr'ythee soon,   915
Even in the passing of thine honey-moon,
Visit my Cytherea: thou wilt find
Cupid well-natured, my Adonis kind;
And pray persuade with thee—Ah, I have done,
All blisses be upon thee, my sweet son!"—   920

102

Thus the fair goddess: while Endymion
Knelt to receive those accents halcyon.

   Meantime a glorious revelry began
Before the Water-Monarch. Nectar ran
In courteous fountains to all cups outreach'd;   925
And plunder'd vines, teeming exhaustless, pleach'd
New growth about each shell and pendent lyre;
The which, in disentangling for their fire,
Pull'd down fresh foliage and coverture
For dainty toying. Cupid, empire-sure,   930
Flutter'd and laugh'd, and oft-times through the throng
Made a delighted way. Then dance, and song,
And garlanding grew wild; and pleasure reign'd.
In harmless tendril they each other chain'd,
And strove who should be smother'd deepest in   935
Fresh crush of leaves.

          O 'tis a very sin
For one so weak to venture his poor verse
In such a place as this. O do not curse,
High Muses! let him hurry to the ending.

   All suddenly were silent. A soft blending   940
Of dulcet instruments came charmingly;
And then a hymn.

       "KING of the stormy sea!
Brother of Jove, and co-inheritor
Of elements! Eternally before
Thee the waves awful bow. Fast, stubborn rock,   945
At thy fear'd trident shrinking, doth unlock
Its deep foundations, hissing into foam.
All mountain-rivers lost, in the wide home

Of thy capacious bosom ever flow.
Thou frownest, and old Eolus thy foe 950
Skulks to his cavern, 'mid the gruff complaint
Of all his rebel tempests. Dark clouds faint
When, from thy diadem, a silver gleam
Slants over blue dominion. Thy bright team
Gulphs in the morning light, and scuds along 955
To bring thee nearer to that golden song
Apollo singeth, while his chariot
Waits at the doors of heaven. Thou art not
For scenes like this: an empire stern hast thou;
And it hath furrow'd that large front: yet now, 960
As newly come of heaven, dost thou sit
To blend and interknit
Subdued majesty with this glad time.
O shell-borne King sublime!
We lay our hearts before thee evermore— 965
We sing, and we adore!

    "Breathe softly, flutes;
Be tender of your strings, ye soothing lutes;
Nor be the trumpet heard! O vain, O vain;
Not flowers budding in an April rain, 970
Nor breath of sleeping dove, nor river's flow,—
No, nor the Eolian twang of Love's own bow,
Can mingle music fit for the soft ear
Of goddess Cytherea!
Yet deign, white Queen of Beauty, thy fair eyes 975
On our souls' sacrifice.

    "Bright-winged Child!
Who has another care when thou hast smil'd?
Unfortunates on earth, we see at last
All death-shadows, and glooms that overcast 980

104

Our spirits, fann'd away by thy light pinions.
O sweetest essence! sweetest of all minions!
God of warm pulses, and dishevell'd hair,
And panting bosoms bare!
Dear unseen light in darkness! eclipser   985
Of light in light! delicious poisoner!
Thy venom'd goblet will we quaff until
We fill—we fill!
And by thy Mother's lips——"

            Was heard no more
For clamour, when the golden palace door   990
Opened again, and from without, in shone
A new magnificence. On oozy throne
Smooth-moving came Oceanus the old,
To take a latest glimpse at his sheep-fold,
Before he went into his quiet cave   995
To muse for ever—Then a lucid wave,
Scoop'd from its trembling sisters of mid-sea,
Afloat, and pillowing up the majesty
Of Doris,[4] and the Egean seer, her spouse—
Next, on a dolphin, clad in laurel boughs,   1000
Theban Amphion leaning on his lute:
His fingers went across it—All were mute
To gaze on Amphitrite, queen of pearls,
And Thetis pearly too.—

            The palace whirls
Around giddy Endymion; seeing he   1005
Was there far strayed from mortality.
He could not bear it—shut his eyes in vain;

---

[4] l. 999 *Doris:* daughter to Oceanus, and wife of the wise Nereus,—named
sometimes the *Aegaean,* as finding in that sea his chief seat of empire.

Imagination gave a dizzier pain.
"O I shall die! sweet Venus, be my stay!
Where is my lovely mistress? Well-away!   1010
I die—I hear her voice—I feel my wing—"
At Neptune's feet he sank. A sudden ring
Of Nereids were about him, in kind strife
To usher back his spirit into life:
But still he slept. At last they interwove   1015
Their cradling arms, and purpos'd to convey
Towards a crystal bower far away.

 Lo! while slow carried through the pitying crowd,
To his inward senses these words spake aloud;
Written in star-light on the dark above: 1020
Dearest Endymion! my entire love!
How have I dwelt in fear of fate: 'tis done—
Immortal bliss for me too hast thou won.
Arise then! for the hen-dove shall not hatch
Her ready eggs, before I'll kissing snatch   1025
Thee into endless heaven. Awake! awake!

 The youth at once arose: a placid lake
Came quiet to his eyes; and forest green,
Cooler than all the wonders he had seen,
Lull'd with its simple song his fluttering breast.   1030
How happy once again in grassy nest!

Endymion

BOOK IV

MUSE of my native land! loftiest Muse!
O first-born on the mountains! by the hues
Of heaven on the spiritual air begot:
Long didst thou sit alone in northern grot,
While yet our England was a wolfish den;   5
Before our forests heard the talk of men;
Before the first of Druids was a child;—
Long didst thou sit amid our regions wild
Rapt in a deep prophetic solitude.
There came an eastern voice of solemn mood:—   10
Yet wast thou patient. Then sang forth the Nine,
Apollo's garland:—yet didst thou divine
Such home-bred glory, that they cry'd in vain,
"Come hither, Sister of the Island!" Plain
Spake fair Ausonia; and once more she spake   15
A higher summons:—still didst thou betake
Thee to thy native hopes. O thou hast won
A full accomplishment! The thing is done,
Which undone, these our latter days had risen
On barren souls. Great Muse, thou know'st what prison 20
Of flesh and bone, curbs, and confines, and frets
Our spirit's wings: despondency besets
Our pillows; and the fresh to-morrow morn
Seems to give forth its light in very scorn
Of our dull, uninspired, snail-paced lives.   25
Long have I said, how happy he who shrives
To thee! But then I thought on poets gone,

And could not pray:—nor can I now—so on
I move to the end in lowliness of heart.——

"Ah, woe is me! that I should fondly part   30
From my dear native land! Ah, foolish maid!
Glad was the hour, when, with thee, myriads bade
Adieu to Ganges and their pleasant fields!
To one so friendless the clear freshet yields
A bitter coolness, the ripe grape is sour: 35
Yet I would have, great gods! but one short hour
Of native air—let me but die at home."

Endymion to heaven's airy dome
Was offering up a hecatomb of vows,
When these words reach'd him. Whereupon he bows   40
His head through thorny-green entanglement
Of underwood, and to the sound is bent,
Anxious as hind towards her hidden fawn.

"Is no one near to help me? No fair dawn
Of life from charitable voice? No sweet saying   45
To set my dull and sadden'd spirit playing?
No hand to toy with mine? No lips so sweet
That I may worship them? No eyelids meet
To twinkle on my bosom? No one dies
Before me, till from these enslaving eyes   50
Redemption sparkles!—I am sad and lost."

Thou, Carian lord, hadst better have been tost
Into a whirlpool. Vanish into air,
Warm mountaineer! for canst thou only bear
A woman's sigh alone and in distress?   55
See not her charms! Is Phoebe passionless?
Phoebe is fairer far—O gaze no more:—

Yet if thou wilt behold all beauty's store,
Behold her panting in the forest grass!
Do not those curls of glossy jet surpass   60
For tenderness the arms so idly lain
Amongst them? Feelest not a kindred pain,
To see such lovely eyes in swimming search
After some warm delight, that seems to perch
Dovelike in the dim cell lying beyond   65
Their upper lids?—Hist!

                "O for Hermes' wand
To touch this flower into human shape!
That woodland Hyacinthus could escape
From his green prison, and here kneeling down
Call me his queen, his second life's fair crown!   70
Ah me, how I could love!—My soul doth melt
For the unhappy youth—Love! I have felt
So faint a kindness, such a meek surrender
To what my own full thoughts had made too tender,
That but for tears my life had fled away!—   75
Ye deaf and senseless minutes of the day,
And thou, old forest, hold ye this for true,
There is no lightning, no authentic dew
But in the eye of love: there's not a sound,
Melodious howsoever, can confound   80
The heavens and earth in one to such a death
As doth the voice of love: there's not a breath
Will mingle kindly with the meadow air,
Till it has panted round, and stolen a share
Of passion from the heart!"—

                Upon a bough   85
He leant, wretched. He surely cannot now
Thirst for another love: O impious,

That he can even dream upon it thus!—
Thought he, "Why am I not as are the dead,
Since to a woe like this I have been led   90
Through the dark earth, and through the wondrous sea?
Goddess! I love thee not the less: from thee
By Juno's smile I turn not—no, no, no—
While the great waters are at ebb and flow.—
I have a triple soul! O fond pretence—   95
For both, for both my love is so immense,
I feel my heart is cut in twain[1] for them."

    And so he groan'd, as one by beauty slain.
The lady's heart beat quick, and he could see
Her gentle bosom heave tumultuously.   100
He sprang from his green covert: there she lay,
Sweet as a muskrose upon new-made hay;
With all her limbs on tremble, and her eyes
Shut softly up alive. To speak he tries.
"Fair damsel, pity me! forgive that I   105
Thus violate thy bower's sanctity!
O pardon me, for I am full of grief—
Grief born of thee, young angel! fairest thief!
Who stolen hast away the wings wherewith
I was to top the heavens. Dear maid, sith   110
Thou art my executioner, and I feel
Loving and hatred, misery and weal,
Will in a few short hours be nothing to me,
And all my story that much passion slew me;
Do smile upon the evening of my days: 115
And, for my tortur'd brain begins to craze,
Be thou my nurse; and let me understand
How dying I shall kiss that lily hand.—

---

[1] l. 97 *in twain* should here, doubtless, follow *for them.*

Dost weep for me? Then should I be content.
Scowl on, ye fates! until the firmament   120
Outblackens Erebus, and the full-cavern'd earth
Crumbles into itself. By the cloud girth
Of Jove, those tears have given me a thirst
To meet oblivion."—As her heart would burst
The maiden sobb'd awhile, and then replied: 125
"Why must such desolation betide
As that thou speakest of? Are not these green nooks
Empty of all misfortune? Do the brooks
Utter a gorgon voice? Does yonder thrush,
Schooling its half-fledg'd little ones to brush   130
About the dewy forest, whisper tales?—
Speak not of grief, young stranger, or cold snails
Will slime the rose to night. Though if thou wilt,
Methinks 'twould be a guilt—a very guilt—
Not to companion thee, and sigh away   135
The light—the dusk—the dark—till break of day!"
"Dear lady," said Endymion, "'tis past:
I love thee! and my days can never last.
That I may pass in patience still speak:
Let me have music dying, and I seek   140
No more delight—I bid adieu to all.
Didst thou not after other climates call,
And murmur about Indian streams?"—Then she,
Sitting beneath the midmost forest tree,
For pity sang this roundelay———   145

          "O Sorrow,
          Why dost borrow
The natural hue of health, from vermeil lips?—
          To give maiden blushes
          To the white rose bushes?   150
Or is it thy dewy hand the daisy tips?

111

"O Sorrow,
Why dost borrow
The lustrous passion from a falcon-eye?—
    To give the glow-worm light?   155
    Or, on a moonless night,
To tinge, on syren shores, the salt sea-spry?

"O Sorrow,
Why dost borrow
The mellow ditties from a mourning tongue?—   160
    To give at evening pale
    Unto the nightingale,
That thou mayst listen the cold dews among?

"O Sorrow,
Why dost borrow   165
Heart's lightness from the merriment of May?—
    A lover would not tread
    A cowslip on the head,
Though he should dance from eve till peep of day—
    Nor any drooping flower   170
    Held sacred for thy bower,
Wherever he may sport himself and play.

"To Sorrow
I bade good-morrow,
And thought to leave her far away behind;   175
    But cheerly, cheerly,
    She loves me dearly;
She is so constant to me, and so kind:
    I would deceive her
    And so leave her,   180
But ah! she is so constant and so kind.

"Beneath my palm trees, by the river side,
I sat a weeping: in the whole world wide
There was no one to ask me why I wept,—
    And so I kept   185
Brimming the water-lily cups with tears
    Cold as my fears.

"Beneath my palm trees, by the river side,
I sat a weeping: what enamour'd bride,
Cheated by shadowy wooer from the clouds,   190
    But hides and shrouds
Beneath dark palm trees by a river side?

"And as I sat, over the light blue hills
There came a noise of revellers: the rills
Into the wide stream came of purple hue—   195
    'Twas Bacchus and his crew!
The earnest trumpet spake, and silver thrills
From kissing cymbals made a merry din—
    'Twas Bacchus and his kin!
Like to a moving vintage down they came,   200
Crown'd with green leaves, and faces all on flame;
All madly dancing through the pleasant valley,
    To scare thee, Melancholy!
O then, O then, thou wast a simple name!
And I forgot thee, as the berried holly   205
By shepherds is forgotten, when, in June,
Tall chesnuts keep away the sun and moon:—
    I rush'd into the folly!

"Within his car, aloft, young Bacchus stood,
Trifling his ivy-dart, in dancing mood,   210
    With sidelong laughing;
And little rills of crimson wine imbrued

His plump white arms, and shoulders, enough white
    For Venus' pearly bite;
And near him rode Silenus on his ass,   215
Pelted with flowers as he on did pass
    Tipsily quaffing.

"Whence came ye, merry Damsels! whence came ye!
So many, and so many, and such glee?
Why have ye left your bowers desolate,   220
    Your lutes, and gentler fate?—
'We follow Bacchus! Bacchus on the wing?
    A conquering!
Bacchus, young Bacchus! good or ill betide,
We dance before him thorough kingdoms wide:— 225
Come hither, lady fair, and joined be
    To our wild minstrelsy!'

"Whence came ye, jolly Satyrs! whence came ye!
So many, and so many, and such glee?
Why have ye left your forest haunts, why left   230
    Your nuts in oak-tree cleft?—
'For wine, for wine we left our kernel tree;
For wine we left our heath, and yellow brooms,
    And cold mushrooms;
For wine we follow Bacchus through the earth; 235
Great God of breathless cups and chirping mirth!—
Come hither, lady fair, and joined be
    To our mad minstrelsy!'

"Over wide streams and mountains great we went,
And, save when Bacchus kept his ivy tent,   240
Onward the tiger and the leopard pants,
    With Asian elephants:
Onward these myriads—with song and dance,

With zebras striped, and sleek Arabians' prance,
Web-footed alligators, crocodiles,   245
Bearing upon their scaly backs, in files,
Plump infant laughers mimicking the coil
Of seamen, and stout galley-rowers' toil:
With toying oars and silken sails they glide,
      Nor care for wind and tide.   250

"Mounted on panthers' furs and lions' manes,
From rear to van they scour about the plains;
A three days' journey in a moment done:
And always, at the rising of the sun,
About the wilds they hunt with spear and horn,   255
      On spleenful unicorn.

"I saw Osirian Egypt kneel adown
      Before the vine-wreath crown!
I saw parch'd Abyssinia rouse and sing
      To the silver cymbals' ring!   260
I saw the whelming vintage hotly pierce
      Old Tartary the fierce!
The kings of Inde their jewel-sceptres vail,
And from their treasures scatter pearled hail;
Great Brahma from his mystic heaven groans,   265
      And all his priesthood moans;
Before young Bacchus' eye-wink turning pale.—
Into these regions came I following him,
Sick hearted, weary—so I took a whim
To stray away into these forests drear   270
      Alone, without a peer:
And I have told thee all thou mayest hear.

     "Young stranger!
     I've been a ranger

In search of pleasure throughout every clime: 275
Alas! 'tis not for me!
Bewitch'd I sure must be,
To lose in grieving all my maiden prime.

"Come then, Sorrow!
Sweetest Sorrow!   280
Like an own babe I nurse thee on my breast:
I thought to leave thee
And deceive thee,
But now of all the world I love thee best.

"There is not one,   285
No, no, not one
But thee to comfort a poor lonely maid;
Thou art her mother,
And her brother,
Her playmate, and her wooer in the shade."   290

O what a sigh she gave in finishing,
And look, quite dead to every worldly thing!
Endymion could not speak, but gazed on her;
And listened to the wind that now did stir
About the crisped oaks full drearily,   295
Yet with as sweet a softness as might be
Remember'd from its velvet summer song.
At last he said: "Poor lady, how thus long
Have I been able to endure that voice?
Fair Melody! kind Syren! I've no choice;   300
I must be thy sad servant evermore:
I cannot choose but kneel here and adore.
Alas, I must not think—by Phoebe, no!
Let me not think, soft Angel! shall it be so?
Say, beautifullest, shall I never think?   305

O thou could'st foster me beyond the brink
Of recollection! make my watchful care
Close up its bloodshot eyes, nor see despair!
Do gently murder half my soul, and I
Shall feel the other half so utterly!—   310
I'm giddy at that cheek so fair and smooth;
O let it blush so ever! let it soothe
My madness! let it mantle rosy-warm
With the tinge of love, panting in safe alarm.—
This cannot be thy hand, and yet it is;   315
And this is sure thine other softling—this
Thine own fair bosom, and I am so near!
Wilt fall asleep? O let me sip that tear!
And whisper one sweet word that I may know
This is this world—sweet dewy blossom!"—*Woe!*   320
Woe! Woe to that Endymion! Where is he?—
Even these words went echoing dismally
Through the wide forest—a most fearful tone,
Like one repenting in his latest moan;
And while it died away a shade pass'd by,   325
As of a thunder cloud. When arrows fly
Through the thick branches, poor ring-doves sleek forth
Their timid necks and tremble; so these both
Leant to each other trembling, and sat so
Waiting for some destruction—when lo,   330
Foot-feather'd Mercury appear'd sublime
Beyond the tall tree tops; and in less time
Than shoots the slanted hail-storm, down he dropt
Towards the ground; but rested not, nor stopt
One moment from his home: only the sward   335
He with his wand light touch'd, and heavenward
Swifter than sight was gone—even before
The teeming earth a sudden witness bore
Of his swift magic. Diving swans appear

Above the crystal circlings white and clear;   340
And catch the cheated eye in wild surprise,
How they can dive in sight and unseen rise—
So from the turf outsprang two steeds jet-black,
Each with large dark blue wings upon his back.
The youth of Caria plac'd the lovely dame   345
On one, and felt himself in spleen to tame
The other's fierceness. Through the air they flew,
High as the eagles. Like two drops of dew
Exhal'd to Phoebus' lips, away they are gone,
Far from the earth away—unseen, alone,   350
Among cool clouds and winds, but that the free,
The buoyant life of song can floating be
Above their heads, and follow them untir'd.—
Muse of my native land, am I inspir'd?
This is the giddy air, and I must spread   355
Wide pinions to keep here; nor do I dread
Or height, or depth, or width, or any chance
Precipitous: I have beneath my glance
Those towering horses and their mournful freight.
Could I thus sail, and see, and thus await   360
Fearless for power of thought, without thine aid?—
There is a sleepy dusk, an odorous shade
From some approaching wonder, and behold
Those winged steeds, with snorting nostrils bold
Snuff at its faint extreme, and seem to tire,   365
Dying to embers from their native fire!

There curl'd a purple mist around them; soon,
It seem'd as when around the pale new moon
Sad Zephyr droops the clouds like weeping willow:
'Twas Sleep slow journeying with head on pillow.   370
For the first time, since he came nigh dead born
From the old womb of night, his cave forlorn

Had he left more forlorn; for the first time,
He felt aloof the day and morning's prime—
Because into his depth Cimmerian   375
There came a dream, shewing how a young man,
Ere a lean bat could plump its wintery skin,
Would at high Jove's empyreal footstool win
An immortality, and how espouse
Jove's daughter, and be reckon'd of his house.   380
Now was he slumbering towards heaven's gate,
That he might at the threshold one hour wait
To hear the marriage melodies, and then
Sink downward to his dusky cave again.
His litter of smooth semilucent mist,   385
Diversely ting'd with rose and amethyst,
Puzzled those eyes that for the centre sought;
And scarcely for one moment could be caught
His sluggish form reposing motionless.
Those two on winged steeds, with all the stress   390
Of vision search'd for him, as one would look
Athwart the sallows of a river nook
To catch a glance at silver throated eels,—
Or from old Skiddaw's top, when fog conceals
His rugged forehead in a mantle pale,   395
With an eye-guess towards some pleasant vale
Descry a favourite hamlet faint and far.

These raven horses, though they foster'd are
Of earth's splenetic fire, dully drop
Their full-veined ears, nostrils blood wide, and stop;   400
Upon the spiritless mist have they outspread
Their ample feathers, are in slumber dead,—
And on those pinions, level in mid air,
Endymion sleepeth and the lady fair.
Slowly they sail, slowly as icy isle   405

Upon a calm sea drifting: and meanwhile
The mournful wanderer dreams. Behold! he walks
On heaven's pavement; brotherly he talks
To divine powers: from his hand full fain
Juno's proud birds are pecking pearly grain: 410
He tries the nerve of Phoebus' golden bow,
And asketh where the golden apples grow:
Upon his arm he braces Pallas' shield,
And strives in vain to unsettle and wield
A Jovian thunderbolt: arch Hebe brings   415
A full-brimm'd goblet, dances lightly, sings
And tantalizes long; at last he drinks,
And lost in pleasure at her feet he sinks,
Touching with dazzled lips her starlight hand.
He blows a bugle,—an ethereal band   420
Are visible above: the Seasons four,—
Green-kyrtled Spring, flush Summer, golden store
In Autumn's sickle, Winter frosty hoar,
Join dance with shadowy Hours; while still the blast,
In swells unmitigated, still doth last   425
To sway their floating morris. "Whose is this?
Whose bugle?" he inquires: they smile—"O Dis!
Why is this mortal here? Dost thou not know
Its mistress' lips? Not thou?—'Tis Dian's: lo!
She rises crescented!" He looks, 'tis she,   430
His very goddess: good-bye earth, and sea,
And air, and pains, and care, and suffering;
Good-bye to all but love! Then doth he spring
Towards her, and awakes—and, strange, o'erhead,
Of those same fragrant exhalations bred,   435
Beheld awake his very dream: the gods
Stood smiling; merry Hebe laughs and nods;
And Phoebe bends towards him crescented.
O state perplexing! On the pinion bed,

Too well awake, he feels the panting side 440
Of his delicious lady. He who died
For soaring too audacious in the sun,
Where that same treacherous wax began to run,
Felt not more tongue-tied than Endymion.
His heart leapt up as to its rightful throne, 445
To that fair shadow'd passion puls'd its way—
Ah, what perplexity! Ah, well a day!
So fond, so beauteous was his bed-fellow,
He could not help but kiss her: then he grew
Awhile forgetful of all beauty save 450
Young Phoebe's, golden hair'd; and so 'gan crave
Forgiveness: yet he turn'd once more to look
At the sweet sleeper,—all his soul was shook,—
She press'd his hand in slumber; so once more
He could not help but kiss her and adore. 455
At this the shadow wept, melting away.
The Latmian started up: "Bright goddess, stay!
Search my most hidden breast! By truth's own tongue,
I have no dædale² heart: why is it wrung
To desperation? Is there nought for me, 460
Upon the bourne of bliss, but misery?"

These words awoke the stranger of dark tresses:
Her dawning love-look rapt Endymion blesses
With 'haviour soft. Sleep yawned from underneath.
"Thou swan of Ganges, let us no more breathe 465
This murky phantasm! thou contented seem'st
Pillow'd in lovely idleness, nor dream'st
What horrors may discomfort thee and me.
Ah, shouldst thou die from my heart-treachery!—
Yet did she merely weep—her gentle soul 470

---

² l. 459 *dædale:* Appears used for *variable.*

121

Hath no revenge in it: as it is whole
In tenderness, would I were whole in love!
Can I prize thee, fair maid, all price above,
Even when I feel as true as innocence?
I do, I do.—What is this soul then? Whence   475
Came it? It does not seem my own, and I
Have no self-passion or identity.
Some fearful end must be: where, where is it?
By Nemesis, I see my spirit flit
Alone about the dark—Forgive me, sweet: 480
Shall we away?" He rous'd the steeds: they beat
Their wings chivalrous into the clear air,
Leaving old Sleep within his vapoury lair.

    The good-night blush of eve was waning slow,
And Vesper, risen star, began to throe[3]   485
In the dusk heavens silvery, when they
Thus sprang direct towards the Galaxy.
Nor did speed hinder converse soft and strange—
Eternal oaths and vows they interchange,
In such wise, in such temper, so aloof   490
Up in the winds, beneath a starry roof,
So witless of their doom, that verily
'Tis well nigh past man's search their hearts to see;
Whether they wept, or laugh'd, or griev'd, or toy'd—
Most like with joy gone mad, with sorrow cloy'd.   495

    Full facing their swift flight, from ebon streak,
The moon put forth a little diamond peak,
No bigger than an unobserved star,
Or tiny point of fairy scymetar;

---

[3] l. 485 *throe:* possibly, to tremble: or, to *throw,* in its sense of twisting and turning.[??]

122

Bright signal that she only stoop'd to tie   500
Her silver sandals, ere deliciously
She bow'd into the heavens her timid head.
Slowly she rose, as though she would have fled,
While to his lady meek the Carian turn'd,
To mark if her dark eyes had yet discern'd   505
This beauty in its birth—Despair! despair!
He saw her body fading gaunt and spare
In the cold moonshine. Straight he seiz'd her wrist;
It melted from his grasp: her hand he kiss'd,
And, horror! kiss'd his own—he was alone.   510
Her steed a little higher soar'd, and then
Dropt hawkwise to the earth.

There lies a den,[4]
Beyond the seeming confines of the space
Made for the soul to wander in and trace
Its own existence, of remotest glooms.   515
Dark regions are around it, where the tombs
Of buried griefs the spirit sees, but scarce
One hour doth linger weeping, for the pierce
Of new-born woe it feels more inly smart:
And in these regions many a venom'd dart   520
At random flies; they are the proper home
Of every ill: the man is yet to come
Who hath not journeyed in this native hell.
But few have ever felt how calm and well
Sleep may be had in that deep den of all.   525
There anguish does not sting; nor pleasure pall:
Woe-hurricanes beat ever at the gate,

---

[4] l. 512–542 This strongly felt and written psychological picture seems to reveal the seriousness of the poet's later years, when the sensuous beauty-world of boyhood was no longer sufficient to distract the soul from the "burthen of the mystery," which no highly-gifted spirit can long escape recognizing.

Yet all is still within and desolate.
Beset with painful gusts, within ye hear
No sound so loud as when on curtain'd bier   530
The death-watch tick is stifled. Enter none
Who strive therefore: on the sudden it is won.
Just when the sufferer begins to burn,
Then it is free to him; and from an urn,
Still fed by melting ice, he takes a draught—   535
Young Semele such richness never quaft
In her maternal longing. Happy gloom!
Dark Paradise! where pale becomes the bloom
Of health by due; where silence dreariest
Is most articulate; where hopes infest;   540
Where those eyes are the brightest far that keep
Their lids shut longest in a dreamless sleep.
O happy spirit-home! O wondrous soul!
Pregnant with such a den to save the whole
In thine own depth. Hail, gentle Carian!   545
For, never since thy griefs and woes began,
Hast thou felt so content: a grievous feud
Hath let thee to this Cave of Quietude.
Aye, his lull'd soul was there, although upborne
With dangerous speed: and so he did not mourn   550
Because he knew not whither he was going.
So happy was he, not the aerial blowing
Of trumpets at clear parley from the east
Could rouse from that fine relish, that high feast.
They stung the feather'd horse: with fierce alarm   555
He flapp'd towards the sound. Alas, no charm
Could lift Endymion's head, or he had view'd
A skyey mask, a pinion'd multitude,—
And silvery was its passing: voices sweet
Warbling the while as if to lull and greet   560

The wanderer in his path. Thus warbled they,
While past the vision went in bright array.

"Who, who from Dian's feast would be away?
For all the golden bowers of the day
Are empty left? Who, who away would be   565
From Cynthia's wedding and festivity?
Not Hesperus: lo! upon his silver wings
He leans away for highest heaven and sings,
Snapping his lucid fingers merrily!—
Ah, Zephyrus! art here, and Flora too!   570
Ye tender bibbers of the rain and dew,
Young playmates of the rose and daffodil,
Be careful, ere ye enter in, to fill
    Your baskets high
With fennel green, and balm, and golden pines,   575
Savory, latter-mint, and columbines,
Cool parsley, basil sweet, and sunny thyme;
Yea, every flower and leaf of every clime,
All gather'd in the dewy morning: hie
    Away! fly, fly!—   580
Crystalline brother of the belt of heaven,
Aquarius! to whom king Jove has given
Two liquid pulse streams 'stead of feather'd wings,
Two fan-like fountains,—thine illuminings
    For Dian play: 585
Dissolve the frozen purity of air;
Let thy white shoulders silvery and bare
Shew cold through watery pinions; make more bright
The Star-Queen's crescent on her marriage night:
    Haste, haste away!—   590
Castor has tamed the planet Lion, see!
And of the Bear has Pollux mastery:
A third is in the race! who is the third,

Speeding away swift as the eagle bird?
   The ramping Centaur!   595
The Lion's mane's on end: the Bear how fierce!
The Centaur's arrow ready seems to pierce
Some enemy: far forth his bow is bent
Into the blue of heaven. He'll be shent,[5]
   Pale unrelentor,   600
When he shall hear the wedding lutes a playing.—
Andromeda! sweet woman! why delaying
So timidly among the stars: come hither!
Join this bright throng, and nimbly follow whither
   They all are going.   605
Danae's Son, before Jove newly bow'd,
Has wept for thee, calling to Jove aloud.
Thee, gentle lady, did he disenthral:
Ye shall for ever live and love, for all
   Thy tears are flowing.—   610
By Daphne's fright, behold Apollo!—"

          More
Endymion heard not: down his steed him bore,
Prone to the green head of a misty hill.

 His first touch of the earth went nigh to kill.
"Alas!" said he, "were I but always borne 615
Through dangerous winds, had but my footsteps worn
A path in hell, for ever would I bless
Horrors which nourish an uneasiness
For my own sullen conquering: to him
Who lives beyond earth's boundary, grief is dim, 620
Sorrow is but a shadow: now I see
The grass; I feel the solid ground—Ah, me!

---

[5] l. 599 *shent:* disgraced.

It is thy voice—divinest! Where?—who? who
Left thee so quiet on this bed of dew?
Behold upon this happy earth we are;   625
Let us ay love each other; let us fare
On forest-fruits, and never, never go
Among the abodes of mortals here below,
Or be by phantoms duped. O destiny!
Into a labyrinth now my soul would fly,   630
But with thy beauty will I deaden it.
Where didst thou melt too? By thee will I sit
For ever: let our fate stop here—a kid
I on this spot will offer: Pan will bid
Us live in peace, in love and peace among   635
His forest wildernesses. I have clung
To nothing, lov'd a nothing, nothing seen
Or felt but a great dream! O I have been
Presumptuous against love, against the sky,
Against all elements, against the tie   640
Of mortals each to each, against the blooms
Of flowers, rush of rivers, and the tombs
Of heroes gone! Against his proper glory
Has my own soul conspired: so my story
Will I to children utter, and repent.   645
There never liv'd a mortal man, who bent
His appetite beyond his natural sphere,
But starv'd and died. My sweetest Indian, here,
Here will I kneel, for thou redeemed hast
My life from too thin breathing: gone and past   650
Are cloudy phantasms. Caverns lone, farewel!
And air of visions, and the monstrous swell
Of visionary seas! No, never more
Shall airy voices cheat me to the shore
Of tangled wonder, breathless and aghast.   655
Adieu, my daintiest Dream! although so vast

My love is still for thee. The hour may come
When we shall meet in pure elysium.
On earth I may not love thee; and therefore
Doves will I offer up, and sweetest store   660
All through the teeming year: so thou wilt shine
On me, and on this damsel fair of mine,
And bless our simple lives. My Indian bliss!
My river-lily bud! one human kiss!
One sigh of real breath—one gentle squeeze,   665
Warm as a dove's nest among summer trees,
And warm with dew at ooze from living blood![6]
Whither didst melt? Ah, what of that!—all good
We'll talk about—no more of dreaming.—Now,
Where shall our dwelling be? Under the brow   670
Of some steep mossy hill, where ivy dun
Would hide us up, although spring leaves were none;
And where dark yew trees, as we rustle through,
Will drop their scarlet berry cups of dew?
O thou wouldst joy to live in such a place;   675
Dusk for our loves, yet light enough to grace
Those gentle limbs on mossy bed reclin'd:
For by one step the blue sky shouldst thou find,
And by another, in deep dell below,
See, through the trees, a little river go   680
All in its mid-day gold and glimmering.
Honey from out the gnarled hive I'll bring,
And apples, wan with sweetness, gather thee,—
Cresses that grow where no man may them see,
And sorrel untorn by the dew-claw'd stag: 685
Pipes will I fashion of the syrinx flag,

---

[6] l. 667 This line presents the single clear trace of experience derived from his medical training which I am aware of, in all the poetry of Keats. The absence of such is remarkable: for anatomy and physiology are fertile in suggestive images, beautiful or powerful, for poetry.

That thou mayst always know whither I roam,
When it shall please thee in our quiet home
To listen and think of love. Still let me speak;
Still let me dive into the joy I seek,— 690
For yet the past doth prison me. The rill,[7]
Thou haply mayst delight in, will I fill
With fairy fishes from the mountain tarn,
And thou shalt feed them from the squirrel's barn.
Its bottom will I strew with amber shells, 695
And pebbles blue from deep enchanted wells.
Its sides I'll plant with dew-sweet eglantine,
And honeysuckles full of clear bee-wine.
I will entice this crystal rill to trace
Love's silver name upon the meadow's face. 700
I'll kneel to Vesta, for a flame of fire;
And to god Phoebus, for a golden lyre;
To Empress Dian, for a hunting spear;
To Vesper, for a taper silver-clear,
That I may see thy beauty through the night; 705
To Flora, and a nightingale shall light
Tame on thy finger; to the River-gods,
And they shall bring thee taper fishing-rods
Of gold, and lines of Naiads' long bright tress.
Heaven shield thee for thine utter loveliness! 710
Thy mossy footstool shall the altar be
'Fore which I'll bend, bending, dear love, to thee:
Those lips shall be my Delphos, and shall speak
Laws to my footsteps, colour to my cheek,
Trembling or stedfastness to this same voice, 715

---

[7] l. 691–710 The sustained flow and clear diction of these beautiful lines,—like those noticed (515–545),—foreshadow the poet's maturest style. There is in this book,—apparently not written in immediate sequence with the preceding,—an ideal character, strangely blended with a few notes of sweet human feeling, which seems to me similarly prelusive.

And of three sweetest pleasurings the choice:
And that affectionate light, those diamond things,
Those eyes, those passions, those supreme pearl springs,
Shall be my grief, or twinkle me to pleasure.
Say, is not bliss within our perfect seisure?   720
O that I could not doubt?"

              The mountaineer
Thus strove by fancies vain and crude to clear
His briar'd path to some tranquillity.
It gave bright gladness to his lady's eye,
And yet the tears she wept were tears of sorrow;   725
Answering thus, just as the golden morrow
Beam'd upward from the vallies of the east:
"O that the flutter of this heart had ceas'd,
Or the sweet name of love had pass'd away.
Young feather'd tyrant! by a swift decay   730
Wilt thou devote this body to the earth:
And I do think that at my very birth
I lisp'd thy blooming titles inwardly;
For at the first, first dawn and thought of thee,
With uplift hands I blest the stars of heaven.   735
Art thou not cruel? Ever have I striven
To think thee kind, but ah, it will not do!
When yet a child, I heard that kisses drew
Favour from thee, and so I kisses gave
To the void air, bidding them find out love: 740
But when I came to feel how far above
All fancy, pride, and fickle maidenhood,
All earthly pleasure, all imagin'd good,
Was the warm tremble of a devout kiss,—
Even then, that moment, at the thought of this,   745
Fainting I fell into a bed of flowers,
And languish'd there three days. Ye milder powers,

Am I not cruelly wrong'd? Believe, believe
Me, dear Endymion, were I to weave
With my own fancies garlands of sweet life,   750
Thou shouldst be one of all. Ah, bitter strife!
I may not be thy love: I am forbidden—
Indeed I am—thwarted, affrighted, chidden,
By things I trembled at, and gorgon wrath.
Twice hast thou ask'd whither I went: henceforth   755
Ask me no more! I may not utter it,
Nor may I be thy love. We might commit
Ourselves at once to vengeance; we might die;
We might embrace and die: voluptuous thought!
Enlarge not to my hunger, or I'm caught   760
In trammels of perverse deliciousness.
No, no, that shall not be: thee will I bless,
And bid a long adieu."

                   The Carian
No word return'd: both lovelorn, silent, wan,
Into the vallies green together went.   765
Far wandering, they were perforce content
To sit beneath a fair lone beechen tree;
Nor at each other gaz'd, but heavily
Por'd on its hazle cirque of shedded leaves.

   Endymion! unhappy! it nigh grieves   770
Me to behold thee thus in last extreme:
Ensky'd ere this, but truly that I deem
Truth the best music in a first-born song.
Thy lute-voic'd brother will I sing ere long,[8]
And thou shalt aid—hast thou not aided me?   775
Yes, moonlight Emperor! felicity

---

[8] l. 774 Alludes, presumably, to *Hyperion*.

131

Has been thy meed for many thousand years;
Yet often have I, on the brink of tears,
Mourn'd as if yet thou wert a forester,—
Forgetting the old tale.

              He did not stir   780
His eyes from the dead leaves, or one small pulse
Of joy he might have felt. The spirit culls
Unfaded amaranth, when wild it strays
Through the old garden-ground of boyish days.
A little onward ran the very stream   785
By which he took his first soft poppy dream;
And on the very bark 'gainst which he leant
A crescent he had carv'd, and round it spent
His skill in little stars. The teeming tree
Had swollen and green'd the pious charactery,   790
But not ta'en out. Why, there was not a slope
Up which he had not fear'd the antelope;
And not a tree, beneath whose rooty shade
He had not with his tamed leopards play'd.
Nor could an arrow light, or javelin,   795
Fly in the air where his had never been—
And yet he knew it not.

             O treachery!
Why does his lady smile, pleasing her eye
With all his sorrowing? He sees her not.
But who so stares on him? His sister sure!   800
Peona of the woods!—Can she endure—
Impossible—how dearly they embrace!
His lady smiles; delight is in her face;
It is no treachery.

"Dear brother mine!
Endymion, weep not so! Why shouldst thou pine   805
When all great Latmos so exalt wilt be?
Thank the great gods, and look not bitterly;
And speak not one pale word, and sigh no more.
Sure I will not believe thou hast such store
Of grief, to last thee to my kiss again.   810
Thou surely canst not bear a mind in pain,
Come hand in hand with one so beautiful.
Be happy both of you! for I will pull
The flowers of autumn for your coronals.
Pan's holy priest for young Endymion calls;   815
And when he is restor'd, thou, fairest dame,
Shalt be our queen. Now, is it not a shame
To see ye thus,—not very, very sad?
Perhaps ye are too happy to be glad:
O feel as if it were a common day;   820
Free-voic'd as one who never was away.
No tongue shall ask, whence come ye? but ye shall
Be gods of your own rest imperial.
Not even I, for one whole month, will pry
Into the hours that have pass'd us by,   825
Since in my arbour I did sing to thee.
O Hermes! on this very night will be
A hymning up to Cynthia, queen of light;
For the soothsayers old saw yesternight
Good visions in the air,—whence will befal,   830
As say these sages, health perpetual
To shepherds and their flocks; and furthermore,
In Dian's face they read the gentle lore:
Therefore for her these vesper-carols are.
Our friends will all be there from nigh and far.   835
Many upon thy death have ditties made;
And many, even now, their foreheads shade

With cypress, on a day of sacrifice.
New singing for our maids shalt thou devise,
And pluck the sorrow from our huntsmen's brows.   840
Tell me, my lady-queen, how to espouse
This wayward brother to his rightful joys!
His eyes are on thee bent, as thou didst poise
His fate most goddess-like. Help me, I pray,
To lure—Endymion, dear brother, say   845
What ails thee?" He could bear no more, and so
Bent his soul fiercely like a spiritual bow,
And twang'd it inwardly, and calmly said:
"I would have thee my only friend, sweet maid!
My only visitor! not ignorant though,   850
That those deceptions which for pleasure go
'Mong men, are pleasures real as real may be:
But there are higher ones I may not see,
If impiously an earthly realm I take.
Since I saw thee, I have been wide awake   855
Night after night, and day by day, until
Of the empyrean I have drunk my fill.
Let it content thee, Sister, seeing me
More happy than betides mortality.
A hermit young, I'll live in mossy cave,   860
Where thou alone shalt come to me, and lave
Thy spirit in the wonders I shall tell.
Through me the shepherd realm shall prosper well;
For to thy tongue will I all health confide.
And, for my sake, let this young maid abide   865
With thee as a dear sister. Thou alone,
Peona, mayst return to me. I own
This may sound strangely: but when, dearest girl,
Thou seest it for my happiness, no pearl
Will trespass down those cheeks. Companion fair!   870
Wilt be content to dwell with her, to share

This sister's love with me?" Like one resign'd
And bent by circumstance, and thereby blind
In self-commitment, thus that meek unknown:
"Aye, but a buzzing by my ears has flown,   875
Of jubilee to Dian:—truth I heard!
Well then, I see there is no little bird,
Tender soever, but is Jove's own care.
Long have I sought for rest, and, unaware,
Behold I find it! so exalted too!   880
So after my own heart! I knew, I knew
There was a place untenanted in it:
In that same void white Chastity shall sit,
And monitor me nightly to lone slumber.
With sanest lips I vow me to the number   885
Of Dian's sisterhood; and, kind lady,
With thy good help, this very night shall see
My future days to her fane consecrate."

    As feels a dreamer what doth most create
His own particular fright, so these three felt: 890
Or like one who, in after ages, knelt
To Lucifer or Baal, when he'd pine
After a little sleep: or when in mine
Far under-ground, a sleeper meets his friends
Who know him not. Each diligently bends   895
Towards common thoughts and things for very fear;
Striving their ghastly malady to cheer,
By thinking it a thing of yes and no,
That housewives talk of. But the spirit-blow
Was struck, and all were dreamers. At the last   900
Endymion said: "Are not our fates all cast?
Why stand we here? Adieu, ye tender pair!
Adieu!" Whereat those maidens, with wild stare,
Walk'd dizzily away. Pained and hot

His eyes went after them, until they got   905
Near to a cypress grove, whose deadly maw,
In one swift moment, would what then he saw
Engulph for ever. "Stay!" he cried, "ah, stay!
Turn, damsels! hist! one word I have to say.
Sweet Indian, I would see thee once again.   910
It is a thing I dote on: so I'd fain,
Peona, ye should hand in hand repair
Into those holy groves, that silent are
Behind great Dian's temple. I'll be yon,
At vesper's earliest twinkle—they are gone—   915
But once, once, once again—" At this he press'd
His hands against his face, and then did rest
His head upon a mossy hillock green,
And so remain'd as he a corpse had been
All the long day; save when he scantly lifted   920
His eyes abroad, to see how shadows shifted
With the slow move of time,—sluggish and weary
Until the poplar tops, in journey dreary,
Had reach'd the river's brim. Then up he rose,
And, slowly as that very river flows,   925
Walk'd towards the temple grove with this lament:
"Why such a golden eve? The breeze is sent
Careful and soft, that not a leaf may fall
Before the serene father of them all
Bows down his summer head below the west.   930
Now am I of breath, speech, and speed possest,
But at the setting I must bid adieu
To her for the last time. Night will strew
On the damp grass myriads of lingering leaves,
And with them shall I die; nor much it grieves   935
To die, when summer dies on the cold sward.
Why, I have been a butterfly, a lord
Of flowers, garlands, love-knots, silly posies,

Groves, meadows, melodies, and arbour roses;
My kingdom's at its death, and just it is   940
That I should die with it: so in all this
We miscal grief, bale, sorrow, heartbreak, woe,
What is there to plain of? By Titan's foe
I am but rightly serv'd." So saying, he
Tripp'd lightly on, in sort of deathful glee;   945
Laughing at the clear stream and setting sun,
As though they jests had been: nor had he done
His laugh at nature's holy countenance,
Until that grove appear'd, as if perchance,
And then his tongue with sober seemlihed   950
Gave utterance as he entered: "Ha!" I said,[9]
"King of the butterflies; but by this gloom,
And by old Rhadamanthus' tongue of doom,
This dusk religion, pomp of solitude,
And the Promethean clay by thief endued,   955
By old Saturnus' forelock, by his head
Shook with eternal palsy, I did wed
Myself to things of light from infancy;
And thus to be cast out, thus lorn to die,
Is sure enough to make a mortal man   960
Grow impious." So he inwardly began
On things for which no wording can be found;
Deeper and deeper sinking, until drown'd
Beyond the reach of music: for the choir
Of Cynthia he heard not, though rough briar   965
Nor muffling thicket interpos'd to dull
The vesper hymn, far swollen, soft and full,
Through the dark pillars of those sylvan aisles.
He saw not the two maidens, nor their smiles,

---

[9] l. 951 *I said*: Endymion here, soliloquizing, refers to the phrase in l. 946, and it
is needless to change the pronoun for "he"

Wan as primroses gather'd at midnight   970
By chilly finger'd spring. "Unhappy wight!
Endymion!" said Peona, "we are here!
What wouldst thou ere we all are laid on bier?"
Then he embrac'd her, and his lady's hand
Press'd, saying:" Sister, I would have command,   975
If it were heaven's will, on our sad fate."
At which that dark-eyed stranger stood elate
And said, in a new voice, but sweet as love,
To Endymion's amaze: "By Cupid's dove,
And so thou shalt! and by the lily truth   980
Of my own breast thou shalt, beloved youth!"
And as she spake, into her face there came
Light, as reflected from a silver flame:
Her long black hair swell'd ampler, in display
Full golden; in her eyes a brighter day   985
Dawn'd blue and full of love. Aye, he beheld
Phoebe, his passion! joyous she upheld
Her lucid bow, continuing thus; "Drear, drear
Has our delaying been; but foolish fear
Withheld me first; and then decrees of fate;   990
And then 'twas fit that from this mortal state
Thou shouldst, my love, by some unlook'd for change
Be spiritualiz'd. Peona, we shall range
These forests, and to thee they safe shall be
As was thy cradle; hither shalt thou flee   995
To meet us many a time." Next Cynthia bright
Peona kiss'd, and bless'd with fair good night:
Her brother kiss'd her too, and knelt adown
Before his goddess, in a blissful swoon.
She gave her fair hands to him, and behold,   1000
Before three swiftest kisses he had told,
They vanish'd far away!—Peona went
Home through the gloomy wood in wonderment.

Lamia

INTRODUCTION

"MY BOOK is coming out," Keats says of this little volume (Summer, 1820), "with very low hopes, though not spirits, on my part. This shall be my last trial;"—Alas! and it was so—: "not succeeding, I shall try what I can do in the apothecary line." With this compare Shelley's remark (Feb. 1821) upon the failure, as he believed, of his *Cenci:* "Nothing is more difficult and unwelcome than to write without a confidence of finding readers."*Lamia,* in hand by July 12, was finished by September 5, 1819. I give these and similar dates, because in the short life and (if the phrase may be admitted) tropical rapidity of growth in the mind and powers of Keats, months count like the years of advance in case of ordinary mortals. *Lamia,* placed first in the volume of 1820, may, however, be considered as his last poem: written "with great care, and after much study of Dryden's versification." "I have great hopes of success," says Keats in his letter of 12 July 1819 "because I make use of my judgment more deliberately than I have yet done, but in case of failure with the world, I shall find my content."

The clear, close narration, and the metre of *Lamia,* reveal at once the influence of Dryden's *Tales:* Keats here freely admits the Alexandrine, and the couplet-structure is much more marked than in *Endymion* or the *Epistles:* while he has admirably found and sustained the balance between a blank-verse treatment of the "Heroic" and the epigrammatic form carried to perfection by Pope. A little of the early mannerism remains: but those overdaring strokes of imaginative diction, those epithets jarringly bold or familiar, which we find in the volumes of 1817 and 1818, have here given place to the secure and lucid touches of masterly art. Details no longer urge themselves forward in lavish and bewildering profusion: the whole is supreme over the parts, every word in its place, and yielding its effect in fulness. The rhyme, in *Endymion* often forced, is managed with an "opulent ease," a Spenserian fluency. *Lamia* leaves on my ear an echo like the delicate richness of Vergil's hexameter in the *Eclogues:* the note of his magical inner sweetness is, in some degree, reached upon a different instrument. I offer this as an illustration, without wishing to press far the parallel between the two great Poets; yet we are reminded of Vergil's grand style by the exquisite skill with which Lamia's love-song (l. 296–300), like that of Silenus in Eclogue VI, is brought in without breaking the current and continuity of the metre.

After the remarks on the Hellenism of Keats in my note upon *Endymion,* it may be enough here to add that *Lamia* is truly Greek in its direct lucidity of phrase, in its touches fresh from Nature, in its descriptive details subordinated to serious human interest. It is Greek also, (though of a lower phase), in its simple sensuousness, which indeed, at times, though rarely, (as in l. 328–333), passes the line of taste: whilst here, also, the *Peris* and *Adam* touch a dissonant chord. Some writers of modern date have gained the praise of being Greek by linguistic turns, quaint archaeological accuracy, or baldness supposed statuesque:—Keats cares for none of these things; so far as he is Greek, he is so by birthright; yet, as mere truthful description, nothing, probably, can be found more true to Hellenic life than such a picture as that given,—l. 350–361—of Colinth at night-fall.

Lamia is, however, essentially "romantic" rather than "classical,"—as the *Eve of St. Agnes* is a frank piece of mediaeval legend.

Poetry more absolutely and triumphantly poetical than these two tales display, I know in no literature: if the estimate may be hazarded, they appear to me emphatically the masterpieces among the Poet's longer   work.

Lamia

PART I

UPON a time, before the faëry broods
Drove Nymph and Satyr from the prosperous woods,
Before King Oberon's bright diadem,
Sceptre, and mantle, clasp'd with dewy gem,
Frighted away the Dryads and the Fauns   5
From rushes green, and brakes, and cowslip'd lawns,
The ever-smitten Hermes empty left
His golden throne, bent warm on amorous theft:
From high Olympus had he stolen light,
On this side of Jove's clouds, to escape the sight   10
Of his great summoner, and made retreat
Into a forest on the shores of Crete.
For somewhere in that sacred island dwelt
A nymph, to whom all hoofed Satyrs knelt;
At whose white feet the languid Tritons poured   15
Pearls, while on land they wither'd and adored.
Fast by the springs where she to bathe was wont,
And in those meads where sometime she might haunt,
Were strewn rich gifts, unknown to any Muse,
Though Fancy's casket were unlock'd to choose.   20
Ah, what a world of love was at her feet!
So Hermes thought, and a celestial heat
Burnt from his winged heels to either ear,
That from a whiteness, as the lily clear,
Blush'd into roses 'mid his golden hair,   25
Fallen in jealous curls about his shoulders bare.

From vale to vale, from wood to wood, he flew,
Breathing upon the flowers his passion new,
And wound with many a river to its head,
To find where this sweet nymph prepar'd her secret bed: 30
In vain; the sweet nymph might nowhere be found,
And so he rested, on the lonely ground,
Pensive, and full of painful jealousies
Of the Wood-Gods, and even the very trees.
There as he stood, he heard a mournful voice,   35
Such as once heard, in gentle heart, destroys
All pain but pity: thus the lone voice spake:
"When from this wreathed tomb shall I awake!
When move in a sweet body fit for life,
And love, and pleasure, and the ruddy strife   40
Of hearts and lips! Ah, miserable me!"
The God, dove-footed, glided silently
Round bush and tree, soft-brushing, in his speed,
The taller grasses and full-flowering weed,
Until he found a palpitating snake,   45
Bright, and cirque-couchant in a dusky brake.

She was a gordian shape of dazzling hue,
Vermilion-spotted, golden, green, and blue;
Striped like a zebra, freckled like a pard,
Eyed like a peacock, and all crimson barr'd;   50
And full of silver moons, that, as she breathed,
Dissolv'd, or brighter shone, or interwreathed
Their lustres with the gloomier tapestries—
So rainbow-sided, touch'd with miseries,
She seem'd, at once, some penanced lady elf,   55
Some demon's mistress, or the demon's self.
Upon her crest she wore a wannish fire
Sprinkled with stars, like Ariadne's tiar:
Her head was serpent, but ah, bitter-sweet!

She had a woman's mouth with all its pearls complete: 60
And for her eyes: what could such eyes do there
But weep, and weep, that they were born so fair?
As Proserpine still weeps for her Sicilian air.
Her throat was serpent, but the words she spake
Came, as through bubbling honey, for Love's sake,   65
And thus; while Hermes on his pinions lay,
Like a stoop'd falcon ere he takes his prey.

"Fair Hermes, crown'd with feathers, fluttering light,
I had a splendid dream of thee last night:
I saw thee sitting, on a throne of gold,   70
Among the Gods, upon Olympus old,
The only sad one; for thou didst not hear
The soft, lute-finger'd Muses chaunting clear,
Nor even Apollo when he sang alone,
Deaf to his throbbing throat's long, long melodious moan.   75
I dreamt I saw thee, robed in purple flakes,
Break amorous through the clouds, as morning breaks,
And, swiftly as a bright Phoebean dart,
Strike for the Cretan isle; and here thou art!
Too gentle Hermes, hast thou found the maid?"   80
Whereat the star of Lethe[1] not delay'd
His rosy eloquence, and thus inquired:
"Thou smooth-lipp'd serpent, surely high inspired!
Thou beauteous wreath, with melancholy eyes,
Possess whatever bliss thou canst devise,   85
Telling me only where my nymph is fled,—
Where she doth breathe!" "Bright planet, thou hast said,"
Return'd the snake, "but seal with oaths, fair God!"
"I swear," said Hermes, "by my serpent rod,

---

[1] l. 81 *the star of Lethe:* Hermes, apparently, is here thus named in allusion to his office of soul-leader from life to Tartarus.

And by thine eyes, and by thy starry crown!"   90
Light flew his earnest words, among the blossoms blown.
Then thus again the brilliance feminine:
"Too frail of heart! for this lost nymph of thine,
Free as the air, invisibly, she strays
About these thornless wilds; her pleasant days   95
She tastes unseen; unseen her nimble feet
Leave traces in the grass and flowers sweet;
From weary tendrils, and bow'd branches green,
She plucks the fruit unseen, she bathes unseen:
And by my power is her beauty veil'd   100
To keep it unaffronted, unassail'd
By the love-glances of unlovely eyes,
Of Satyrs, Fauns, and blear'd Silenus' sighs.
Pale grew her immortality, for woe
Of all these lovers, and she grieved so   105
I took compassion on her, bade her steep
Her hair in weird syrops, that would keep
Her loveliness invisible, yet free
To wander as she loves, in liberty.
"Thou shalt behold her, Hermes, thou alone,   110
If thou wilt, as thou swearest, grant my boon!"
Then, once again, the charmed God began
An oath, and through the serpent's ears it ran
Warm, tremulous, devout, psalterian.
Ravish'd, she lifted her Circean head,   115
Blush'd a live damask, and swift-lisping said,
"I was a woman, let me have once more
A woman's shape, and charming as before.
I love a youth of Corinth—O the bliss!
Give me my woman's form, and place me where he is.   120
Stoop, Hermes, let me breathe upon thy brow,
And thou shalt see thy sweet nymph even now."
The God on half-shut feathers sank serene,

She breath'd upon his eyes, and swift was seen
Of both the guarded nymph near-smiling on the green.   125
It was no dream; or say a dream it was,
Real are the dreams of Gods, and smoothly pass
Their pleasures in a long immortal dream.
One warm, flush'd moment, hovering, it might seem
Dash'd by the wood-nymph's beauty, so he burn'd;   130
Then, lighting on the printless verdure, turn'd
To the swoon'd serpent, and with languid arm,
Delicate, put to proof the lythe Caducean charm.
So done, upon the nymph his eyes he bent,
Full of adoring tears and blandishment,   135
And towards her stept: she, like a moon in wane,
Faded before him, cower'd, nor could restrain
Her fearful sobs, self-folding like a flower
That faints into itself at evening hour:
But the God fostering her chilled hand,   140
She felt the warmth, her eyelids open'd bland,
And, like new flowers at morning song of bees,
Bloom'd, and gave up her honey to the lees.
Into the green-recessed woods they flew;
Nor grew they pale, as mortal lovers do.   145

   Left to herself, the serpent now began
To change; her elfin blood in madness ran,
Her mouth foam'd, and the grass, therewith besprent,
Wither'd at dew so sweet and virulent;
Her eyes in torture fix'd, and anguish drear,   150
Hot, glaz'd, and wide, with lid-lashes all sear,
Flash'd phosphor and sharp sparks, without one cooling tear.
The colours all inflam'd throughout her train,
She writh'd about, convuls'd with scarlet pain:
A deep volcanian yellow took the place   155
Of all her milder-mooned body's grace;

And, as the lava ravishes the mead,
Spoilt all her silver mail, and golden brede;
Made gloom of all her frecklings, streaks and bars,
Eclips'd her crescents, and lick'd up her stars: 160
So that, in moments few, she was undrest
Of all her sapphires, greens, and amethyst,
And rubious-argent: of all these bereft,
Nothing but pain and ugliness were left.
Still shone her crown; that vanish'd, also she   165
Melted and disappear'd as suddenly;
And in the air, her new voice luting soft,
Cried, "Lycius! gentle Lycius!"—Borne aloft
With the bright mists about the mountains hoar
These words dissolv'd: Crete's forests heard no more.   170

Whither fled Lamia,[2] now a lady bright,
A full-born beauty new and exquisite?
She fled into that valley they pass o'er
Who go to Corinth from Cenchreas' shore;
And rested at the foot of those wild hills,   175
The rugged founts of the Peraean rills,
And of that other ridge whose barren back
Stretches, with all its mist and cloudy rack,
South-westward to Cleone. There she stood
About a young bird's flutter from a wood,   180
Fair, on a sloping green of mossy tread,
By a clear pool, wherein she passioned
To see herself escap'd from so sore ills,
While her robes flaunted with the daffodils.

---

[2] l. 171 *Whither fled Lamia:* Cenchrêae is a seaport on the south side of the Isthmus of Corinth: the Peraea, a mountainous district to north-west. Cleone lies to the southward.

Ah, happy Lycius!—for she was a maid   185
More beautiful than ever twisted braid,
Or sigh'd, or blush'd, or on spring-flowered lea
Spread a green kirtle to the minstrelsy:
A virgin purest lipp'd, yet in the lore
Of love deep learned to the red heart's core: 190
Not one hour old, yet of sciential brain
To unperplex bliss from its neighbour pain;
Define their pettish limits, and estrange
Their points of contact, and swift counterchange;
Intrigue with the specious chaos, and dispart   195
Its most ambiguous atoms with sure art;
As though in Cupid's college she had spent
Sweet days a lovely graduate, still unshent,[3]
And kept his rosy terms in idle languishment.

  Why this fair creature chose so faërily   200
By the wayside to linger, we shall see;
But first 'tis fit to tell how she could muse
And dream, when in the serpent prison-house,
Of all she list, strange or magnificent:
How, ever, where she will'd, her spirit went;   205
Whether to faint Elysium, or where
Down through tress-lifting waves the Nereids fair
Wind into Thetis' bower by many a pearly stair;
Or where God Bacchus drains his cups divine,
Stretch'd out, at ease, beneath a glutinous pine;   210
Or where in Pluto's gardens palatine
Mulciber's columns gleam in far piazzian line.
And sometimes into cities she would send
Her dream, with feast and rioting to blend;

---

[3] l. 198 *unshent:* Keats here seems to use this, one of his favourite old words, as
equivalent to *maiden.*

And once, while among mortals dreaming thus,   215
She saw the young Corinthian Lycius
Charioting foremost in the envious race,
Like a young Jove with calm uneager face,
And fell into a swooning love of him.
Now on the moth-time of that evening dim   220
He would return that way, as well she knew,
To Corinth from the shore; for freshly blew
The eastern soft wind, and his galley now
Grated the quaystones with her brazen prow
In port Cenchreas, from Egina isle   225
Fresh anchor'd; whither he had been awhile
To sacrifice to Jove, whose temple there
Waits with high marble doors for blood and incense rare.
Jove heard his vows, and better'd his desire;
For by some freakful chance he made retire   230
From his companions, and set forth to walk,
Perhaps grown wearied of their Corinth talk:
Over the solitary hills he fared,
Thoughtless at first, but ere eve's star appeared
His phantasy was lost, where reason fades,   235
In the calm'd twilight of Platonic shades.
Lamia beheld him coming, near, more near—
Close to her passing, in indifference drear,
His silent sandals swept the mossy green;
So neighbour'd to him, and yet so unseen   240
She stood: he pass'd, shut up in mysteries,
His mind wrapp'd like his mantle, while her eyes
Follow'd his steps, and her neck regal white
Turn'd—syllabling thus, "Ah, Lycius bright,
And will you leave me on the hills alone?   245
Lycius, look back! and be some pity shown."
He did; not with cold wonder fearingly,
But Orpheus-like at an Eurydice;

For so delicious were the words she sung,
It seem'd he had lov'd them a whole summer long:　　　250
And soon his eyes had drunk her beauty up,
Leaving no drop in the bewildering cup,
And still the cup was full,—while he afraid
Lest she should vanish ere his lip had paid
Due adoration, thus began to adore;　　　255
Her soft look growing coy, she saw his chain so sure:
"Leave thee alone! Look back! Ah, Goddess, see
Whether my eyes can ever turn from thee!
For pity do not this sad heart belie—
Even as thou vanishest so I shall die.　　　260
Stay! though a Naiad of the rivers, stay!
To thy far wishes will thy streams obey:
Stay! though the greenest woods be thy domain,
Alone they can drink up the morning rain:
Though a descended Pleiad, will not one　　　265
Of thine harmonious sisters keep in tune
Thy spheres, and as thy silver proxy shine?
So sweetly to these ravish'd ears of mine
Came thy sweet greeting, that if thou shouldst fade
Thy memory will waste me to a shade:—　　　270
For pity do not melt!"—"If I should stay,"
Said Lamia, "here, upon this floor of clay,
And pain my steps upon these flowers too rough,
What canst thou say or do of charm enough
To dull the nice remembrance of my home?　　　275
Thou canst not ask me with thee here to roam
Over these hills and vales, where no joy is,—
Empty of immortality and bliss!
Thou art a scholar, Lycius, and must know
That finer spirits cannot breathe below　　　280
In human climes, and live: Alas! poor youth,
What taste of purer air hast thou to soothe

My essence? What serener palaces,
Where I may all my many senses please,
And by mysterious sleights a hundred thirsts appease?   285
It cannot be—Adieu!" So said, she rose
Tiptoe with white arms spread. He, sick to lose
The amorous promise of her lone complain,
Swoon'd, murmuring of love, and pale with pain.
The cruel lady, without any show   290
Of sorrow for her tender favourite's woe,
But rather, if her eyes could brighter be,
With brighter eyes and slow amenity,
Put her new lips to his, and gave afresh
The life she had so tangled in her mesh: 295
And as he from one trance was wakening
Into another, she began to sing,
Happy in beauty, life, and love, and every thing,
A song of love, too sweet for earthly lyres,
While, like held breath, the stars drew in their panting fires 300
And then she whisper'd in such trembling tone,
As those who, safe together met alone
For the first time through many anguish'd days,
Use other speech than looks; bidding him raise
His drooping head, and clear his soul of doubt,   305
For that she was a woman, and without
Any more subtle fluid in her veins
Than throbbing blood, and that the self-same pains
Inhabited her frail-strung heart as his.
And next she wonder'd how his eyes could miss   310
Her face so long in Corinth, where, she said,
She dwelt but half retir'd, and there had led
Days happy as the gold coin could invent
Without the aid of love; yet in content
Till she saw him, as once she pass'd him by,   315
Where 'gainst a column he leant thoughtfully

At Venus' temple porch, 'mid baskets heap'd
Of amorous herbs and flowers, newly reap'd
Late on that eve, as 'twas the night before
The Adonian feast; whereof she saw no more,   320
But wept alone those days, for why should she adore?
Lycius from death awoke into amaze,
To see her still, and singing so sweet lays;
Then from amaze into delight he fell
To hear her whisper woman's lore so well;   325
And every word she spake entic'd him on
To unperplex'd delight and pleasure known.
Let the mad poets say whate'er they please
Of the sweets of Fairies, Peris, Goddesses,
There is not such a treat among them all,   330
Haunters of cavern, lake, and waterfall,
As a real woman, lineal indeed
From Pyrrha's pebbles or old Adam's seed.
Thus gentle Lamia judg'd, and judg'd aright,
That Lycius could not love in half a fright,   335
So threw the goddess off, and won his heart
More pleasantly by playing woman's part,
With no more awe than what her beauty gave,
That, while it smote, still guaranteed to save.
Lycius to all made eloquent reply,   340
Marrying to every word a twinborn sigh;
And last, pointing to Corinth, ask'd her sweet,
If 'twas too far that night for her soft feet.
The way was short, for Lamia's eagerness
Made, by a spell, the triple league decrease   345
To a few paces; not at all surmised
By blinded Lycius, so in her comprized.
They pass'd the city gates, he knew not how
So noiseless, and he never thought to know.

As men talk in a dream, so Corinth all,   350
Throughout her palaces imperial,
And all her populous streets and temples lewd,
Mutter'd, like tempest in the distance brew'd,
To the wide-spreaded night above her towers.
Men, women, rich and poor, in the cool hours,   355
Shuffled their sandals o'er the pavement white,
Companion'd or alone; while many a light
Flared, here and there, from wealthy festivals,
And threw their moving shadows on the walls,
Or found them cluster'd in the corniced shade   360
Of some arch'd temple door, or dusky colonnade.

Muffling his face, of greeting friends in fear,
Her fingers he press'd hard, as one came near
With curl'd gray beard, sharp eyes, and smooth bald crown,
Slow-stepp'd, and robed in philosophic gown: 365
Lycius shrank closer, as they met and past,
Into his mantle, adding wings to haste,
While hurried Lamia trembled: "Ah," said he,
"Why do you shudder, love, so ruefully?
Why does your tender palm dissolve in dew?"—   370
"I'm wearied," said fair Lamia: "tell me who
Is that old man? I cannot bring to mind
His features:—Lycius! wherefore did you blind
Yourself from his quick eyes?" Lycius replied,
"'Tis Apollonius sage, my trusty guide   375
And good instructor; but to-night he seems
The ghost of folly haunting my sweet dreams."

While yet he spake they had arrived before
A pillar'd porch, with lofty portal door,
Where hung a silver lamp, whose phosphor glow   380
Reflected in the slabbed steps below,

Mild as a star in water; for so new,
And so unsullied was the marble hue,
So through the crystal polish, liquid fine,
Ran the dark veins, that none but feet divine   385
Could e'er have touch'd there. Sounds Aeolian
Breath'd from the hinges, as the ample span
Of the wide doors disclos'd a place unknown
Some time to any, but those two alone,
And a few Persian mutes, who that same year   390
Were seen about the markets: none knew where
They could inhabit; the most curious
Were foil'd, who watch'd to trace them to their house:
And but the flitter-winged verse must tell,
For truth's sake, what woe afterwards befel,   395
'Twould humour many a heart to leave them thus,
Shut from the busy world of more incredulous.

Lamia

PART II

LOVE in a hut, with water and a crust,
Is—Love, forgive us!—cinders, ashes, dust;
Love in a palace is perhaps at last
More grievous torment than a hermit's fast:—
That is a doubtful tale from faery land,   5
Hard for the non-elect to understand.
Had Lycius liv'd to hand his story down,
He might have given the moral a fresh frown,
Or clench'd it quite: but too short was their bliss
To breed distrust and hate, that make the soft voice hiss.   10
Besides, there, nightly, with terrific glare,
Love, jealous grown of so complete a pair,
Hover'd and buzz'd his wings, with fearful roar,
Above the lintel of their chamber door,
And down the passage cast a glow upon the floor.   15

For all this came a ruin: side by side
They were enthroned, in the even tide,
Upon a couch, near to a curtaining
Whose airy texture, from a golden string,
Floated into the room, and let appear   20
Unveil'd the summer heaven, blue and clear,
Betwixt two marble shafts:—there they reposed,
Where use had made it sweet, with eyelids closed,
Saving a tythe which love still open kept,
That they might see each other while they almost slept;   25
When from the slope side of a suburb hill,
Deafening the swallow's twitter, came a thrill

Of trumpets—Lycius started—the sounds fled,
But left a thought, a buzzing in his head.
For the first time, since first he harbour'd in   30
That purple-lined palace of sweet sin,
His spirit pass'd beyond its golden bourn
Into the noisy world almost forsworn.
The lady, ever watchful, penetrant,
Saw this with pain, so arguing a want   35
Of something more, more than her empery
Of joys; and she began to moan and sigh
Because he mused beyond her, knowing well
That but a moment's thought is passion's passing bell.
"Why do you sigh, fair creature?" whisper'd he: 40
"Why do you think?" return'd she tenderly:
"You have deserted me;—where am I now?
Not in your heart while care weighs on your brow:
No, no, you have dismiss'd me; and I go
From your breast houseless: ay, it must be so."   45
He answer'd, bending to her open eyes,
Where he was mirror'd small in paradise,
"My silver planet, both of eve and morn!
Why will you plead yourself so sad forlorn,
While I am striving how to fill my heart   50
With deeper crimson, and a double smart?
How to entangle, trammel up and snare
Your soul in mine, and labyrinth you there
Like the hid scent in an unbudded rose?
Ay, a sweet kiss—you see your mighty woes.   55
My thoughts! shall I unveil them? Listen then!
What mortal hath a prize, that other men
May be confounded and abash'd withal,
But lets it sometimes pace abroad majestical,
And triumph, as in thee I should rejoice   60
Amid the hoarse alarm of Corinth's voice.

Let my foes choke, and my friends shout afar,
While through the thronged streets your bridal car
Wheels round its dazzling spokes."—The lady's cheek
Trembled; she nothing said, but, pale and meek,   65
Arose and knelt before him, wept a rain
Of sorrows at his words; at last with pain
Beseeching him, the while his hand she wrung,
To change his purpose. He thereat was stung,
Perverse, with stronger fancy to reclaim   70
Her wild and timid nature to his aim:
Besides, for all his love, in self despite,
Against his better self, he took delight
Luxurious in her sorrows, soft and new.
His passion, cruel grown, took on a hue   75
Fierce and sanguineous as 'twas possible
In one whose brow had no dark veins to swell.
Fine was the mitigated fury, like
Apollo's presence when in act to strike
The serpent—Ha, the serpent! certes, she   80
Was none. She burnt, she lov'd the tyranny,
And, all subdued, consented to the hour
When to the bridal he should lead his paramour.
Whispering in midnight silence, said the youth,
"Sure some sweet name thou hast, though, by my truth,   85
"I have not ask'd it, ever thinking thee
Not mortal, but of heavenly progeny,
As still I do. Hast any mortal name,
Fit appellation for this dazzling frame?
Or friends or kinsfolk on the citied earth,   90
To share our marriage feast and nuptial mirth?"
"I have no friends," said Lamia, "no, not one;
My presence in wide Corinth hardly known:
My parents' bones are in their dusty urns
Sepulchred, where no kindled incense burns,   95

Seeing all their luckless race are dead, save me,
And I neglect the holy rite for thee.
Even as you list invite your many guests;
But if, as now it seems, your vision rests
With any pleasure on me, do not bid   100
Old Apollonius—from him keep me hid."
Lycius, perplex'd at words so blind and blank,
Made close inquiry; from whose touch she shrank,
Feigning a sleep; and he to the dull shade
Of deep sleep in a moment was betray'd.   105

   It was the custom then to bring away
The bride from home at blushing shut of day,
Veil'd, in a chariot, heralded along
By strewn flowers, torches, and a marriage song,
With other pageants: but this fair unknown   110
Had not a friend. So being left alone,
(Lycius was gone to summon all his kin)
And knowing surely she could never win
His foolish heart from its mad pompousness,
She set herself, high-thoughted, how to dress   115
The misery in fit magnificence.
She did so, but 'tis doubtful how and whence
Came, and who were her subtle servitors.
About the halls, and to and from the doors,
There was a noise of wings, till in short space   120
The glowing banquet-room shone with wide-arched grace.
A haunting music, sole perhaps and lone
Supportress of the faery-roof, made moan
Throughout, as fearful the whole charm might fade.
Fresh carved cedar, mimicking a glade   125
Of palm and plantain, met from either side,
High in the midst, in honour of the bride:
Two palms and then two plantains, and so on,

From either side their stems branch'd one to one
All down the aisled place; and beneath all   130
There ran a stream of lamps straight on from wall to wall.
So canopied, lay an untasted feast
Teeming with odours. Lamia, regal drest,
Silently paced about, and as she went,
In pale contented sort of discontent,   135
Mission'd her viewless servants to enrich
The fretted splendour of each nook and niche.
Between the tree-stems, marbled plain at first,
Came jasper pannels; then, anon, there burst
Forth creeping imagery of slighter trees,   140
And with the larger wove in small intricacies.
Approving all, she faded at self-will,
And shut the chamber up, close, hush'd and still,
Complete and ready for the revels rude,
When dreadful guests would come to spoil her solitude.   145

    The day appear'd, and all the gossip rout.
O senseless Lycius! Madman! wherefore flout
The silent-blessing fate, warm cloister'd hours,
And show to common eyes these secret bowers?
The herd approach'd; each guest, with busy brain,   150
Arriving at the portal, gaz'd amain,
And enter'd marveling: for they knew the street,
Remember'd it from childhood all complete
Without a gap, yet ne'er before had seen
That royal porch, that high-built fair demesne;   155
So in they hurried all, maz'd, curious and keen:
Save one, who look'd thereon with eye severe,
And with calm-planted steps walk'd in austere;
'Twas Apollonius: something too he laugh'd,
As though some knotty problem, that had daft   160
His patient thought, had now begun to thaw,

And solve and melt:—'twas just as he foresaw.

He met within the murmurous vestibule
His young disciple. "'Tis no common rule,
Lycius," said he, "for uninvited guest   165
To force himself upon you, and infest
With an unbidden presence the bright throng
Of younger friends; yet must I do this wrong,
And you forgive me." Lycius blush'd, and led
The old man through the inner doors broad-spread;   170
With reconciling words and courteous mien
Turning into sweet milk the sophist's spleen.

Of wealthy lustre was the banquet-room,
Fill'd with pervading brilliance and perfume:
Before each lucid pannel fuming stood   175
A censer fed with myrrh and spiced wood,
Each by a sacred tripod held aloft,
Whose slender feet wide-swerv'd upon the soft
Wool-woofed carpets: fifty wreaths of smoke
From fifty censers their light voyage took   180
To the high roof, still mimick'd as they rose
Along the mirror'd walls by twin-clouds odorous.
Twelve sphered tables, by silk seats insphered,
High as the level of a man's breast rear'd
On libbard's paws, upheld the heavy gold   185
Of cups and goblets, and the store thrice told
Of Ceres' horn, and, in huge vessels, wine
Came from the gloomy tun with merry shine.
Thus loaded with a feast the tables stood,
Each shrining in the midst the image of a God.   190

When in an antichamber every guest
Had felt the cold full sponge to pleasure press'd,

By minist'ring slaves, upon his hands and feet,
And fragrant oils with ceremony meet
Pour'd on his hair, they all mov'd to the feast   195
In white robes, and themselves in order placed
Around the silken couches, wondering
Whence all this mighty cost and blaze of wealth could spring.

Soft went the music the soft air along,
While fluent Greek a vowel'd undersong   200
Kept up among the guests discoursing low
At first, for scarcely was the wine at flow;
But when the happy vintage touch'd their brains,
Louder they talk, and louder come the strains
Of powerful instruments:—the gorgeous dyes,   205
The space, the splendour of the draperies,
The roof of awful richness, nectarous cheer,
Beautiful slaves, and Lamia's self, appear,
Now, when the wine has done its rosy deed,
And every soul from human trammels freed,   210
No more so strange; for merry wine, sweet wine,
Will make Elysian shades not too fair, too divine.
Soon was God Bacchus at meridian height;
Flush'd were their cheeks, and bright eyes double bright:
Garlands of every green, and every scent   215
From vales deflower'd, or forest-trees branch rent,
In baskets of bright osier'd gold were brought
High as the handles heap'd, to suit the thought
Of every guest; that each, as he did please,
Might fancy-fit his brows, silk-pillow'd at his ease.   220

What wreath for Lamia? What for Lycius?
What for the sage, old Apollonius?
Upon her aching forehead be there hung
The leaves of willow and of adder's tongue;

And for the youth, quick, let us strip for him   225
The thyrsus, that his watching eyes may swim
Into forgetfulness; and, for the sage,
Let spear-grass and the spiteful thistle wage
War on his temples. Do not all charms fly
At the mere touch of cold philosophy?   230
There was an awful rainbow once in heaven:
We know her woof, her texture; she is given
In the dull catalogue of common things.
Philosophy will clip an Angel's wings,
Conquer all mysteries by rule and line,   235
Empty the haunted air, and gnomed mine—
Unweave a rainbow, as it erewhile made
The tender-person'd Lamia melt into a shade.

    By her glad Lycius sitting, in chief place,
Scarce saw in all the room another face,   240
Till, checking his love trance, a cup he took
Full brimm'd, and opposite sent forth a look
'Cross the broad table, to beseech a glance
From his old teacher's wrinkled countenance,
And pledge him. The bald-head philosopher   245
Had fix'd his eye, without a twinkle or stir
Full on the alarmed beauty of the bride,
Brow-beating her fair form, and troubling her sweet pride.
Lycius then press'd her hand, with devout touch,
As pale it lay upon the rosy couch: 250
'Twas icy, and the cold ran through his veins;
Then sudden it grew hot, and all the pains
Of an unnatural heat shot to his heart.
"Lamia, what means this? Wherefore dost thou start?
Know'st thou that man?" Poor Lamia answer'd not.   255
He gaz'd into her eyes, and not a jot
Own'd they the lovelorn piteous appeal:

More, more he gaz'd: his human senses reel:
Some hungry spell that loveliness absorbs;
There was no recognition in those orbs.   260
"Lamia!" he cried—and no soft-toned reply.
The many heard, and the loud revelry
Grew hush; the stately music no more breathes;
The myrtle sicken'd in a thousand wreaths.
By faint degrees, voice, lute, and pleasure ceased;   265
A deadly silence step by step increased,
Until it seem'd a horrid presence there,
And not a man but felt the terror in his hair.
"Lamia!" he shriek'd; and nothing but the shriek
With its sad echo did the silence break.   270
"Begone, foul dream!" he cried, gazing again
In the bride's face, where now no azure vein
Wander'd on fair-spaced temples; no soft bloom
Misted the cheek; no passion to illume
The deep-recessed vision:—all was blight;   275
Lamia, no longer fair, there sat a deadly white.
"Shut, shut those juggling eyes, thou ruthless man!
Turn them aside, wretch! or the righteous ban
Of all the Gods, whose dreadful images
Here represent their shadowy presences,   280
May pierce them on the sudden with the thorn
Of painful blindness; leaving thee forlorn,
In trembling dotage to the feeblest fright
Of conscience, for their long offended might,
For all thine impious proud-heart sophistries,   285
Unlawful magic, and enticing lies.
Corinthians! look upon that gray-beard wretch!
Mark how, possess'd, his lashless eyelids stretch
Around his demon eyes! Corinthians, see!
My sweet bride withers at their potency."   290
"Fool!" said the sophist, in an under-tone

Gruff with contempt; which a death-nighing moan
From Lycius answer'd, as heart-struck and lost,
He sank supine beside the aching ghost.
"Fool! Fool!" repeated he, while his eyes still   295
Relented not, nor mov'd; "from every ill
Of life have I preserv'd thee to this day,
And shall I see thee made a serpent's prey?
Then Lamia breath'd death breath; the sophist's eye,
Like a sharp spear, went through her utterly,   300
Keen, cruel, perceant, stinging: she, as well
As her weak hand could any meaning tell,
Motion'd him to be silent; vainly so,
He look'd and look'd again a level—No!
"A Serpent!" echoed he; no sooner said,   305
Than with a frightful scream she vanished:
And Lycius' arms were empty of delight,
As were his limbs of life, from that same night.
On the high couch he lay!—his friends came round—
Supported him—no pulse, or breath they found,   310
And, in its marriage robe, the heavy body wound.[1]

---

[1] "Philostratus, in his fourth book *de Vita Apollonii*, hath a memorable instance in this kind, which I may not omit, of one Menippus Lycius,a young man twenty-five years of age, that going betwixt Cenchreas and Corinth, met such a phantasm in the habit of a fair gentlewoman, which taking him by the hand, carried him home to her house, in the suburbs of Corinth, and told him she was a Phoenician by birth, and if he would tarry with her, he should hear her sing and play, and drink such wine as never any drank, and no man should molest him; but she, being fair and lovely, would live and die with him, that was fair and lovely to behold. The young man, a philosopher, otherwise staid and discreet, able to moderate his passions, though not this of love, tarried with her awhile to his great content, and at last married her, to whose wedding, amongst other guests, came Apollonius; who, by some probable conjectures, found her out to be a serpent, a lamia; and that all her furniture was, like Tantalus' gold, described by Homer, no substance, but mere illusions. When she saw herself descried, she wept, and desired Apollonius to be silent, but he would not be moved, and thereupon she, plate, house, and all that was in it, vanished in an instant; many thousands took notice of this fact, for it was done in the midst of Greece." — Burton's *Anatomy of Melancholy*, Part 3, Sect. 2, Memb. I. Subs. I.

Isabella,

or the Pot of Basil

A Story from Boccaccio

INTRODUCTION

FINISHED by 27 Ap. 1818, at Teignmouth. The source is Boccaccio's *Decamerone,* Gior. iv, Nov. 5, where the tale is placed in the mouth of Philomena. But the story, rather baldly told, is without the fine detail, the touches of character, the depth of sentiment,—the poetry, in short, with which Keats has clothed it. In st. xix he makes a graceful apology for his enlargement of the original theme by the episode upon Isabella's brothers and their trading ventures. Boccaccio, true to his usual creeping morality, treats their conduct to Lorenzo as a piece of natural common sense.—The old literary superstition, (analogous to that which placed Ariosto among the supreme poets, or Guido among the supreme painters, of the world), clinging still about Boccaccio, influenced Leigh Hunt, and, probably through him, Keats. But although the *Decamerone* had great value in its own day as a masterwork in style, singularly graceful and lucid in point of narrative diction, yet it really contains very few stories which, even looking to bare plan and form, have any poetical merit: whilst in his moralization and the general character of his tales, Boccaccio is own brother to Polonius. Even the skill and taste of Keats have not here fully succeeded in turning the coarse, physical motives common to the *Decamerone* and other mediaeval stories, into beauty. Yet the pathos and picturesqueness of the whole is such that we have no reason to regret that song upon the fate of the lovers which, (according to Philomena), "anchora hoggi si canta,"—in Naples or Messina.

Isabella

I

FAIR Isabel, poor simple Isabel!
  Lorenzo, a young palmer in Love's eye!
They could not in the self-same mansion dwell
  Without some stir of heart, some malady;
They could not sit at meals but feel how well   5
  It soothed each to be the other by;
They could not, sure, beneath the same roof sleep
But to each other dream, and nightly weep.

II

With every morn their love grew tenderer,
  With every eve deeper and tenderer still;   10
He might not in house, field, or garden stir,
  But her full shape would all his seeing fill;
And his continual voice was pleasanter
  To her, than noise of trees or hidden rill;
Her lute-string gave an echo of his name,   15
She spoilt her half-done broidery with the same.

III

He knew whose gentle hand was at the latch,
  Before the door had given her to his eyes;
And from her chamber-window he would catch
  Her beauty farther than the falcon spies;   20
And constant as her vespers would he watch,
  Because her face was turn'd to the same skies;
And with sick longing all the night outwear,
To hear her morning-step upon the stair.

IV

A whole long month of May in this sad plight   25
   Made their cheeks paler by the break of June:
"To morrow will I bow to my delight,
   To-morrow will I ask my lady's boon."—
"O may I never see another night,
   Lorenzo, if thy lips breathe not love's tune."—   30
So spake they to their pillows; but, alas,
Honeyless days and days did he let pass;

V

Until sweet Isabella's untouch'd cheek
   Fell sick within the rose's just domain,
Fell thin as a young mother's, who doth seek   35
   By every lull to cool her infant's pain:
"How ill she is," said he, "I may not speak,
   And yet I will, and tell my love all plain:
If looks speak love-laws, I will drink her tears,
And at the least 'twill startle off her cares."   40

VI

So said he one fair morning, and all day
   His heart beat awfully against his side;
And to his heart he inwardly did pray
   For power to speak; but still the ruddy tide
Stifled his voice, and puls'd resolve away—   45
   Fever'd his high conceit of such a bride,
Yet brought him to the meekness of a child:
Alas! when passion is both meek and wild!

VII

So once more he had wak'd and anguished
   A dreary night of love and misery,   50

If Isabel's quick eye had not been wed
    To every symbol on his forehead high;
She saw it waxing very pale and dead,
    And straight all flush'd; so, lisped tenderly,
"Lorenzo!"—here she ceas'd her timid quest,   55
But in her tone and look he read the rest.

VIII

"O Isabella, I can half perceive
    That I may speak my grief into thine ear;
If thou didst ever any thing believe,
    Believe how I love thee, believe how near   60
My soul is to its doom: I would not grieve
    Thy hand by unwelcome pressing, would not fear
Thine eyes by gazing; but I cannot live
Another night, and not my passion shrive.

IX

"Love! thou art leading me from wintry cold,   65
    Lady! thou leadest me to summer clime,
And I must taste the blossoms that unfold
    In its ripe warmth this gracious morning time."
So said, his erewhile timid lips grew bold,
    And poesied with hers in dewy rhyme: 70
Great bliss was with them, and great happiness
Grew, like a lusty flower in June's caress.[1]

X

Parting they seem'd to tread upon the air,
    Twin roses by the zephyr blown apart

---

[1] st. ix Some overcolour, some overpressure of the phrase remains here: so in st. xiii:—Keats has not yet reached the self-restraint and clearness of his latest work. But the rhyme is very rarely forced.

Only to meet again more close, and share 75
    The inward fragrance of each other's heart.
She, to her chamber gone, a ditty fair
    Sang, of delicious love and honey'd dart;
He with light steps went up a western hill,
And bade the sun farewell, and joy'd his fill. 80

XI

All close they met again, before the dusk
    Had taken from the stars its pleasant veil,
All close they met, all eves, before the dusk
    Had taken from the stars its pleasant veil,
Close in a bower of hyacinth and musk, 85
    Unknown of any, free from whispering tale.
Ah! better had it been for ever so,
Than idle ears should pleasure in their woe.

XII

Were they unhappy then?—It cannot be—
    Too many tears for lovers have been shed, 90
Too many sighs give we to them in fee,
    Too much of pity after they are dead,
Too many doleful stories do we see,
    Whose matter in bright gold were best be read;
Except in such a page where Theseus' spouse 95
Over the pathless waves towards him bows.

XIII

But, for the general award of love,
    The little sweet doth kill much bitterness;
Though Dido silent is in under-grove,
    And Isabella's was a great distress, 100
Though young Lorenzo in warm Indian clove

Was not embalm'd, this truth is not the less—
Even bees, the little almsmen of spring-bowers,
Know there is richest juice in poison-flowers.

XIV

With her two brothers this fair lady dwelt,   105
    Enriched from ancestral merchandize,
And for them many a weary hand did swelt
    In torched mines and noisy factories,
And many once proud-quiver'd loins did melt
    In blood from stinging whip;—with hollow eyes   110
Many all day in dazzling river stood,
To take the rich-ored driftings of the flood.

XV

For them the Ceylon diver held his breath,
    And went all naked to the hungry shark;
For them his ears gush'd blood; for them in death   115
    The seal on the cold ice with piteous bark
Lay full of darts; for them alone did seethe
    A thousand men in troubles wide and dark:
Half-ignorant, they turn'd an easy wheel,
That set sharp racks at work, to pinch and peel.   120

XVI

Why were they proud? Because their marble founts
    Gush'd with more pride than do a wretch's tears?—
Why were they proud? Because fair orange-mounts
    Were of more soft ascent than lazar stairs?—
Why were they proud? Because red-lin'd accounts   125
    Were richer than the songs of Grecian years?—
Why were they proud? again we ask aloud,
Why in the name of Glory were they proud?

XVII

Yet were these Florentines as self-retired
    In hungry pride and gainful cowardice,   130
As two close Hebrews in that land inspired,
    Paled in and vineyarded from beggar-spies,
The hawks of ship-mast forests—the untired
    And pannier'd mules for ducats and old lies—
Quick cat's-paws on the generous stray-away,—   135
Great wits in Spanish, Tuscan, and Malay.[2]

XVIII

How was it these same ledger-men could spy
    Fair Isabella in her downy nest?
How could they find out in Lorenzo's eye
    A straying from his toil? Hot Egypt's pest   140
Into their vision covetous and sly!
    How could these money-bags see east and west?—
Yet so they did—and every dealer fair
Must see behind, as doth the hunted hare.

XIX

O eloquent and famed Boccaccio!   145
    Of thee we now should ask forgiving boon,
And of thy spicy myrtles as they blow,
    And of thy roses amorous of the moon,
And of thy lilies, that do paler grow
    Now they can no more hear thy ghittern's tune,   150
For venturing syllables that ill beseem
The quiet glooms of such a piteous theme.

---

[2] st. xvi, xvii The general sense of these stanzas is more intelligible than the expression, in which closeness and condensation pass into obscurity. *Hawks of the shipmast forests* I take to be, Ready to pounce on the trading-vessels as they come in: *Malay,* Oriental trade in general.

XX

Grant thou a pardon here, and then the tale
    Shall move on soberly, as it is meet;
There is no other crime, no mad assail   155
    To make old prose in modern rhyme more sweet:
But it is done—succeed the verse or fail—
    To honour thee, and thy gone spirit greet;
To stead thee as a verse in English tongue,
An echo of thee in the north-wind sung.   160

XXI

These brethren having found by many signs
    What love Lorenzo for their sister had,
And how she lov'd him too, each unconfines
    His bitter thoughts to other, well nigh mad
That he, the servant of their trade designs,   165
    Should in their sister's love be blithe and glad,
When 'twas their plan to coax her by degrees
To some high noble and his olive-trees.

XXII

And many a jealous conference had they,
    And many times they bit their lips alone,   170
Before they fix'd upon a surest way
    To make the youngster for his crime atone;
And at the last, these men of cruel clay
    Cut Mercy with a sharp knife to the bone;
For they resolved in some forest dim   175
To kill Lorenzo, and there bury him.

XXIII

So on a pleasant morning, as he leant
    Into the sun-rise, o'er the balustrade

Of the garden-terrace, towards him they bent
   Their footing through the dews; and to him said,   180
"You seem there in the quiet of content,
   Lorenzo, and we are most loth to invade
Calm speculation; but if you are wise,
Bestride your steed while cold is in the skies.

XXIV

"To-day we purpose, ay, this hour we mount   185
   To spur three leagues towards the Apennine;
Come down, we pray thee, ere the hot sun count
   His dewy rosary on the eglantine."
Lorenzo, courteously as he was wont,
   Bow'd a fair greeting to these serpents' whine;   190
And went in haste, to get in readiness,
With belt, and spur, and bracing huntsman's dress.

XXV

And as he to the court-yard pass'd along,
   Each third step did he pause, and listen'd oft
If he could hear his lady's matin-song,   195
   Or the light whisper of her footstep soft;
And as he thus over his passion hung,
   He heard a laugh full musical aloft;
When, looking up, he saw her features bright
Smile through an in-door lattice, all delight.   200

XXVI

"Love, Isabel!" said he, "I was in pain
   Lest I should miss to bid thee a good morrow:
Ah! what if I should lose thee, when so fain
   I am to stifle all the heavy sorrow
Of a poor three hours' absence? but we'll gain   205

Out of the amorous dark what day doth borrow.
Good bye! I'll soon be back."—"Good bye!" said she:—
And as he went she chanted merrily.

XXVII

So the two brothers and their murder'd man
    Rode past fair Florence, to where Arno's stream   210
Gurgles through straiten'd banks, and still doth fan
    Itself with dancing bulrush, and the bream
Keeps head against the freshets. Sick and wan
    The brothers' faces in the ford did seem,
Lorenzo's flush with love.—They pass'd the water   215
Into a forest quiet for the slaughter.

XXVIII

There was Lorenzo slain and buried in,
    There in that forest did his great love cease;
Ah! when a soul doth thus its freedom win,
    It aches in loneliness—is ill at peace   220
As the break-covert blood-hounds of such sin:
    They dipp'd their swords in the water, and did tease
Their horses homeward, with convulsed spur,
Each richer by his being a murderer.

XXIX

They told their sister how, with sudden speed,   225
    Lorenzo had ta'en ship for foreign lands,
Because of some great urgency and need
    In their affairs, requiring trusty hands.
Poor Girl! put on thy stifling widow's weed,
    And 'scape at once from Hope's accursed bands;   230
To-day thou wilt not see him, nor to-morrow,
And the next day will be a day of sorrow.

XXX

She weeps alone for pleasures not to be;
    Sorely she wept until the night came on,
And then, instead of love, O misery!   235
    She brooded o'er the luxury alone:
His image in the dusk she seem'd to see,
    And to the silence made a gentle moan,
Spreading her perfect arms upon the air,
And on her couch low murmuring, "Where? O where?"   240

XXXI

But Selfishness, Love's cousin, held not long
    Its fiery vigil in her single breast;
She fretted for the golden hour, and hung
    Upon the time with feverish unrest—
Not long—for soon into her heart a throng   245
    Of higher occupants, a richer zest,
Came tragic; passion not to be subdued,
And sorrow for her love in travels rude.

XXXII

In the mid days of autumn, on their eves
    The breath of Winter comes from far away,   250
And the sick west continually bereaves
    Of some gold tinge, and plays a roundelay
Of death among the bushes and the leaves,
    To make all bare before he dares to stray
From his north cavern. So sweet Isabel   255
By gradual decay from beauty fell,

XXXIII

Because Lorenzo came not. Oftentimes
    She ask'd her brothers, with an eye all pale,

Striving to be itself, what dungeon climes
    Could keep him off so long? They spake a tale   260
Time after time, to quiet her. Their crimes
    Came on them, like a smoke from Hinnom's vale;
And every night in dreams they groan'd aloud,
To see their sister in her snowy shroud.

XXXIV

And she had died in drowsy ignorance,   265
    But for a thing more deadly dark than all;
It came like a fierce potion, drunk by chance,
    Which saves a sick man from the feather'd pall
For some few gasping moments; like a lance,
    Waking an Indian from his cloudy hall   270
With cruel pierce, and bringing him again
Sense of the gnawing fire at heart and brain.

XXXV

It was a vision.—In the drowsy gloom,
    The dull of midnight, at her couch's foot
Lorenzo stood, and wept: the forest tomb   275
    Had marr'd his glossy hair which once could shoot
Lustre into the sun, and put cold doom
    Upon his lips, and taken the soft lute
From his lorn voice, and past his loamed ears
Had made a miry channel for his tears.   280

XXXVI

Strange sound it was, when the pale shadow spake;
    For there was striving, in its piteous tongue,
To speak as when on earth it was awake,
    And Isabella on its music hung:
Languor there was in it, and tremulous shake,   285

As in a palsied Druid's harp unstrung;
And through it moan'd a ghostly under-song,
Like hoarse night-gusts sepulchral briars among.

XXXVII

Its eyes, though wild, were still all dewy bright
    With love, and kept all phantom fear aloof   290
From the poor girl by magic of their light,
    The while it did unthread the horrid woof
Of the late darken'd time,—the murderous spite
    Of pride and avarice,—the dark pine roof
In the forest,—and the sodden turfed dell,   295
Where, without any word, from stabs he fell.

XXXVIII

Saying moreover, "Isabel, my sweet!
    Red whortle-berries droop above my head,
And a large flint-stone weighs upon my feet;
    Around me beeches and high chestnuts shed   300
Their leaves and prickly nuts; a sheep-fold bleat
    Comes from beyond the river to my bed:
Go, shed one tear upon my heather-bloom,
And it shall comfort me within the tomb.

XXXIX

"I am a shadow now, alas! alas!   305
    Upon the skirts of human-nature dwelling
Alone: I chant alone the holy mass,
    While little sounds of life are round me knelling,
And glossy bees at noon do fieldward pass,
    And many a chapel bell the hour is telling,   310
Paining me through: those sounds grow strange to me,
And thou art distant in Humanity.

XL

"I know what was, I feel full well what is,
  And I should rage, if spirits could go mad;
Though I forget the taste of earthly bliss,   315
  That paleness warms my grave, as though I had
A Seraph chosen from the bright abyss
  To be my spouse: thy paleness makes me glad;
Thy beauty grows upon me, and I feel
A greater love through all my essence steal."   320

XLI

The Spirit mourn'd "Adieu!"—dissolv'd, and left
  The atom darkness in a slow turmoil;
As when of healthful midnight sleep bereft,
  Thinking on rugged hours and fruitless toil,
We put our eyes into a pillowy cleft,   325
  And see the spangly gloom froth up and boil:
It made sad Isabella's eyelids ache,
And in the dawn she started up awake;

XLII

"Ha! ha!" said she, "I knew not this hard life,
  I thought the worst was simple misery;   330
I thought some Fate with pleasure or with strife
  Portion'd us—happy days, or else to die;
But there is crime—a brother's bloody knife!
  Sweet Spirit, thou hast school'd my infancy:
I'll visit thee for this, and kiss thine eyes,   335
And greet thee morn and even in the skies."

XLIII

When the full morning came, she had devised
  How she might secret to the forest hie;

How she might find the clay, so dearly prized,
　　And sing to it one latest lullaby;　　　　　　　　340
How her short absence might be unsurmised,
　　While she the inmost of the dream would try.
Resolv'd, she took with her an aged nurse,
And went into that dismal forest-hearse.

XLIV

See, as they creep along the river side,　　　　　　345
　　How she doth whisper to that aged Dame,
And, after looking round the champaign wide,
　　Shows her a knife.—"What feverous hectic flame
Burns in thee, child?—What good can thee betide,
　　That thou should'st smile again?"—The evening came,
And they had found Lorenzo's earthy bed;　　　　351
The flint was there, the berries at his head.

XLV

Who hath not loiter'd in a green church-yard,
　　And let his spirit, like a demon-mole,
Work through the clayey soil and gravel hard,　　355
　　To see skull, coffin'd bones, and funeral stole;
Pitying each form that hungry Death hath marr'd,
　　And filling it once more with human soul?
Ah! this is holiday to what was felt
When Isabella by Lorenzo knelt.　　　　　　　360

XLVI

She gaz'd into the fresh-thrown mould, as though
　　One glance did fully all its secrets tell;
Clearly she saw, as other eyes would know
　　Pale limbs at bottom of a crystal well;
Upon the murderous spot she seem'd to grow,　　365

Like to a native lily of the dell:
Then with her knife, all sudden, she began
To dig more fervently than misers can.

XLVII

Soon she turn'd up a soiled glove, whereon
    Her silk had play'd in purple phantasies,   370
She kiss'd it with a lip more chill than stone,
    And put it in her bosom, where it dries
And freezes utterly unto the bone
    Those dainties made to still an infant's cries:
Then 'gan she work again; nor stay'd her care,   375
But to throw back at times her veiling hair.

XLVIII

That old nurse stood beside her wondering,
    Until her heart felt pity to the core
At sight of such a dismal labouring,
    And so she kneeled, with her locks all hoar,   380
And put her lean hands to the horrid thing:
    Three hours they labour'd at this travail sore;
At last they felt the kernel of the grave,
And Isabella did not stamp and rave.

XLIX

Ah! wherefore all this wormy circumstance?   385
    Why linger at the yawning tomb so long?
O for the gentleness of old Romance,
    The simple plaining of a minstrel's song!
Fair reader, at the old tale take a glance,
    For here, in truth, it doth not well belong   390
To speak:—O turn thee to the very tale,
And taste the music of that vision pale.

L

With duller steel than the Persèan sword[3]
    They cut away no formless monster's head,
But one, whose gentleness did well accord   395
    With death, as life. The ancient harps have said,
Love never dies, but lives, immortal Lord:
    If Love impersonate was ever dead,
Pale Isabella kiss'd it, and low moan'd.
'Twas love; cold,—dead indeed, but not dethroned.   400

LI

In anxious secrecy they took it home,
    And then the prize was all for Isabel:
She calm'd its wild hair with a golden comb,
    And all around each eye's sepulchral cell
Pointed each fringed lash; the smeared loam   405
    With tears, as chilly as a dripping well,
She drench'd away:—and still she comb'd, and kept
Sighing all day—and still she kiss'd, and wept.

LII

Then in a silken scarf,—sweet with the dews
    Of precious flowers pluck'd in Araby,   410
And divine liquids come with odorous ooze
    Through the cold serpent pipe refreshfully,—
She wrapp'd it up; and for its tomb did choose
    A garden-pot, wherein she laid it by,
And cover'd it with mould, and o'er it set   415
Sweet Basil, which her tears kept ever wet.

---

[3] st. l, l. 1 *the Persèan sword:* Perseus, the slayer of Medusa.

LIII

And she forgot the stars, the moon, and sun,
   And she forgot the blue above the trees,
And she forgot the dells where waters run,
   And she forgot the chilly autumn breeze;   420
She had no knowledge when the day was done,
   And the new morn she saw not: but in peace
Hung over her sweet Basil evermore,
And moisten'd it with tears unto the core.

LIV

And so she ever fed it with thin tears,   425
   Whence thick, and green, and beautiful it grew,
So that it smelt more balmy than its peers
   Of Basil-tufts in Florence; for it drew
Nurture besides, and life, from human fears,
   From the fast mouldering head there shut from view:
So that the jewel, safely casketed,   431
Came forth, and in perfumed leafits[4] spread.

LV

O Melancholy, linger here awhile!
   O Music, Music, breathe despondingly!
O Echo, Echo, from some sombre isle,   435
   Unknown, Lethean, sigh to us—O sigh!
Spirits in grief, lift up your heads, and smile;
   Lift up your heads, sweet Spirits, heavily,
And make a pale light in your cypress glooms,
Tinting with silver wan your marble tombs.   440

---

[4] st. liv, l. 8 *leafits:* In this pretty diminutive, (whether borrowed by Keats or coined), the analogy of *floweret* may have been followed.

187

LVI

Moan hither, all ye syllables of woe,
    From the deep throat of sad Melpomene!
Through bronzed lyre in tragic order go,
    And touch the strings into a mystery;
Sound mournfully upon the winds and low;   445
    For simple Isabel is soon to be
Among the dead: She withers, like a palm
Cut by an Indian for its juicy balm.

LVII

O leave the palm to wither by itself;
    Let not quick Winter chill its dying hour!—   450
It may not be—those Baalites of pelf,
    Her brethren, noted the continual shower
From her dead eyes; and many a curious elf,
    Among her kindred, wonder'd that such dower
Of youth and beauty should be thrown aside   455
By one mark'd out to be a Noble's bride.

LVIII

And, furthermore, her brethren wonder'd much
    Why she sat drooping by the Basil green,
And why it flourish'd, as by magic touch;
    Greatly they wonder'd what the thing might mean: 460
They could not surely give belief, that such
    A very nothing would have power to wean
Her from her own fair youth, and pleasures gay,
And even remembrance of her love's delay.

LIX

Therefore they watch'd a time when they might sift 465
    This hidden whim; and long they watch'd in vain;

For seldom did she go to chapel-shrift,
    And seldom felt she any hunger-pain;
And when she left, she hurried back, as swift
    As bird on wing to breast its eggs again;   470
And, patient as a hen-bird, sat her there
Beside her Basil, weeping through her hair.

LX

Yet they contriv'd to steal the Basil-pot,
    And to examine it in secret place:
The thing was vile with green and livid spot,   475
    And yet they knew it was Lorenzo's face:
The guerdon of their murder they had got,
    And so left Florence in a moment's space,
Never to turn again.—Away they went,
With blood upon their heads, to banishment.   480

LXI

O Melancholy, turn thine eyes away!
    O Music, Music, breathe despondingly!
O Echo, Echo, on some other day,
    From isles Lethean, sigh to us—O sigh!
Spirits of grief, sing not your "Well-a-way!"   485
    For Isabel, sweet Isabel, will die;
Will die a death too lone and incomplete,
Now they have ta'en away her Basil sweet.

LXII

Piteous she look'd on dead and senseless things,
    Asking for her lost Basil amorously: 490
And with melodious chuckle in the strings
    Of her lorn voice, she oftentimes would cry
After the Pilgrim in his wanderings,

To ask him where her Basil was; and why
'Twas hid from her: "For cruel 'tis," said she,   495
"To steal my Basil-pot away from me."

LXIII

And so she pined, and so she died forlorn,
    Imploring for her Basil to the last.
No heart was there in Florence but did mourn
    In pity of her love, so overcast.   500
And a sad ditty of this story born
    From mouth to mouth through all the country pass'd:
Still is the burthen sung—"O cruelty,
    To steal my Basil-pot away from me!"

The Eve of
St. Agnes

INTRODUCTION

KEATS, doubtless, was indebted for his subject to Brand's "Popular Antiquities," 1795. "On the eve of her day," 21 Jan., that writer says, "many kinds of divination were practised by virgins to discover their future husbands." He cites some lines, assigned to Ben Jonson, upon the subject, and refers to Burton's "Anatomy of Melancholy," as speaking of *"Maids fasting on St. Agnes' Eve,* to know who shall be their first husband." A long quotation from an old chap-book then gives the legend in detail;—furnishing obviously the outline of our poem.

St. Agnes' wool (st. xiii) is that shorn from two lambs which, (allusive to the Saint's name), were upon that day brought to Mass, and offered whilst the *Agnus* was chanted. The wool was then spun, dressed, and woven by the hand of Nuns.

It is, apparently, as a poetical contrast to the fasting which was generally accepted as the due method by which a maiden was to prepare herself for the Vision, that the gorgeous supper-picture of st. xxx was introduced. Keats, who was Leigh Hunt's guest at the time when this volume appeared, read aloud the passage to Hunt, with manifest pleasure in his work:—the sole instance I can recall when the poet,—modest in proportion to his greatness,—yielded even to so innocent an impulse of vanity.

A fine remark by Mr. A. de Vere upon the *Faerie Queene* is equally applicable to this Poem, and also to *Lamia:*—"The gift of delineating beauty finds perhaps its most arduous triumph when exercised on the description of *incident,* a thing that passes necessarily from change to change,—and not on permanent objects, which less elude the artist's eye and hand."

"There is a tendency to class women in my books with roses and sweetmeats,—they never see themselves dominant," said Keats, (about Aug. 1820), alluding to a report that his last book was unpopular among them. This remark applies, perhaps, most to the *Eve of St. Agnes.* Keats did not live long enough to attain,—as, despite his own criticism, many passages in his poems show that he would have attained,—the standard of his great Master, of whom Professor Dowden truly notes that "For Spenser, behind each woman made to worship or love, rises a sacred presence—Womanhood itself."

This magnificent poem was written by Feb., and revised in Sep. 1819.

The Eve of St. Agnes

I

ST. AGNES' Eve—Ah, bitter chill it was!
The owl, for all his feathers, was a-cold;
The hare limp'd trembling through the frozen grass,
And silent was the flock in woolly fold:
Numb were the Beadsman's fingers, while he told   5
His rosary, and while his frosted breath,
Like pious incense from a censer old,
Seem'd taking flight for heaven, without a death,
Past the sweet Virgin's picture, while his prayer he saith.

II.

His prayer he saith, this patient, holy man;   10
Then takes his lamp, and riseth from his knees,
And back returneth, meagre, barefoot, wan,
Along the chapel aisle by slow degrees:
The sculptur'd dead, on each side, seem to freeze,
Emprison'd in black, purgatorial rails: 15
Knights, ladies, praying in dumb orat'ries,
He passeth by; and his weak spirit fails
To think how they may ache in icy hoods and mails.

III.

Northward he turneth through a little door,
And scarce three steps, ere Music's golden tongue   20
Flatter'd to tears this aged man and poor;
But no—already had his deathbell rung;
The joys of all his life were said and sung:
His was harsh penance on St. Agnes' Eve:

Another way he went, and soon among   25
Rough ashes sat he for his soul's reprieve,
And all night kept awake, for sinners' sake to grieve.

IV.

That ancient Beadsman heard the prelude soft;
And so it chanc'd, for many a door was wide,
From hurry to and fro. Soon, up aloft,   30
The silver, snarling trumpets 'gan to chide:
The level chambers, ready with their pride,
Were glowing to receive a thousand guests:
The carved angels, ever eager-eyed,
Star'd, where upon their heads the cornice rests,   35
With hair blown back, and wings put cross-wise on their breasts.

V.

At length burst in the argent revelry,
With plume, tiara, and all rich array,
Numerous as shadows haunting fairily
The brain, new stuff d, in youth, with triumphs gay   40
Of old romance. These let us wish away,
And turn, sole-thoughted, to one Lady there,
Whose heart had brooded, all that wintry day,
On love, and wing'd St. Agnes' saintly care,
As she had heard old dames full many times declare.   45

VI.

They told her how, upon St. Agnes' Eve,
Young virgins might have visions of delight,
And soft adorings from their loves receive
Upon the honey'd middle of the night,
If ceremonies due they did aright;   50
As, supperless to bed they must retire,

And couch supine their beauties, lily white;
Nor look behind, nor sideways, but require
Of Heaven with upward eyes for all that they desire.

VII.

Full of this whim was thoughtful Madeline: 55
The music, yearning like a God in pain,
She scarcely heard: her maiden eyes divine,
Fix'd on the floor, saw many a sweeping train
Pass by—she heeded not at all: in vain
Came many a tiptoe, amorous cavalier,   60
And back retir'd; not cool'd by high disdain,
But she saw not: her heart was otherwhere:
She sigh'd for Agnes' dreams, the sweetest of the year.[1]

VIII.

She danc'd along with vague, regardless eyes,
Anxious her lips, her breathing quick and short: 65
The hallow'd hour was near at hand: she sighs
Amid the timbrels, and the throng'd resort
Of whisperers in anger, or in sport;
'Mid looks of love, defiance, hate, and scorn,
Hoodwink'd with faery fancy; all amort,   70
Save to St. Agnes and her lambs unshorn,
And all the bliss to be before to-morrow morn.

IX.

So, purposing each moment to retire,
She linger'd still. Meantime, across the moors,
Had come young Porphyro, with heart on fire   75

---

[1] st. vi–viii The mode in which Keats,—that Elizabethan born out of due time,—here and elsewhere, as in *Isabella,* "dallies with the innocence of love, Like the old age," seems to me rather the naïvetè of Mediaevalism than that of Antiquity.

For Madeline. Beside the portal doors,
Buttress'd from moonlight, stands he, and implores
All saints to give him sight of Madeline,
But for one moment in the tedious hours,
That he might gaze and worship all unseen;   80
Perchance speak, kneel, touch, kiss—in sooth such things have been.

X.

He ventures in: let no buzz'd whisper tell:
All eyes be muffled, or a hundred swords
Will storm his heart, Love's fev'rous citadel:
For him, those chambers held barbarian hordes,   85
Hyena foemen, and hot-blooded lords,
Whose very dogs would execrations howl
Against his lineage: not one breast affords
Him any mercy, in that mansion foul,
Save one old beldame, weak in body and in soul.   90

XI.

Ah, happy chance! the aged creature came,
Shuffling along with ivory-headed wand,
To where he stood, hid from the torch's flame,
Behind a broad hail-pillar, far beyond
The sound of merriment and chorus bland: 95
He startled her; but soon she knew his face,
And grasp'd his fingers in her palsied hand,
Saying, "Mercy, Porphyro! hie thee from this place;
"They are all here to-night, the whole blood-thirsty race!

XII.

"Get hence! get hence! there's dwarfish Hildebrand;   100
He had a fever late, and in the fit
He cursed thee and thine, both house and land:

Then there 's that old Lord Maurice, not a whit
More tame for his gray hairs—Alas me! flit!
Flit like a ghost away."—"Ah, Gossip dear,   105
We're safe enough; here in this arm-chair sit,
And tell me how"—"Good Saints! not here, not here;
Follow me, child, or else these stones will be thy bier."

XIII.

He follow'd through a lowly arched way,
Brushing the cobwebs with his lofty plume;   110
And as she mutter'd "Well-a—well-a-day!"
He found him in a little moonlight room,
Pale, lattic'd, chill, and silent as a tomb.
"Now tell me where is Madeline," said he,
"O tell me, Angela, by the holy loom   115
Which none but secret sisterhood may see,
When they St. Agnes' wool are weaving piously."

XIV.

"St. Agnes! Ah! it is St. Agnes' Eve—
Yet men will murder upon holy days:
Thou must hold water in a witch's sieve,   120
And be liege-lord of all the Elves and Fays,
To venture so: it fills me with amaze
To see thee, Porphyro!—St. Agnes' Eve!
God's help! my lady fair the conjuror plays
This very night: good angels her deceive!   125
But let me laugh awhile, I've mickle time to grieve."

XV.

Feebly she laugheth in the languid moon,
While Porphyro upon her face doth look,
Like puzzled urchin on an aged crone

Who keepeth clos'd a wond'rous riddle-book,   130
As spectacled she sits in chimney nook.
But soon his eyes grew brilliant, when she told
His lady's purpose; and he scarce could brook
Tears, at the thought of those enchantments cold,
And Madeline asleep in lap of legends old.   135

XVI.

Sudden a thought came like a full-blown rose,
Flushing his brow, and in his pained heart
Made purple riot: then doth he propose
A stratagem, that makes the beldame start:
"A cruel man and impious thou art: 140
Sweet lady, let her pray, and sleep, and dream
Alone with her good angels, far apart
From wicked men like thee. Go, go!—I deem
Thou canst not surely be the same that thou didst seem.

XVII.

"I will not harm her, by all saints I swear,"   145
Quoth Porphyro: "O may I ne'er find grace
When my weak voice shall whisper its last prayer,
If one of her soft ringlets I displace,
Or look with ruffian passion in her face:
Good Angela, believe me by these tears;   150
Or I will, even in a moment's space,
Awake, with horrid shout, my foemen's ears,
And beard them, though they be more fang'd than wolves and bears."

XVIII.

"Ah! why wilt thou affright a feeble soul?
A poor, weak, palsy-stricken, churchyard thing,   155
Whose passing-bell may ere the midnight toll;

Whose prayers for thee, each morn and evening,
Were never miss'd."—Thus plaining, doth she bring
A gentler speech from burning Porphyro;
So woful, and of such deep sorrowing,   160
That Angela gives promise she will do
Whatever he shall wish, betide her weal or woe.

XIX.

Which was, to lead him, in close secrecy,
Even to Madeline's chamber, and there hide
Him in a closet, of such privacy   165
That he might see her beauty unespied,
And win perhaps that night a peerless bride,
While legion'd fairies pac'd the coverlet,
And pale enchantment held her sleepy-eyed.
Never on such a night have lovers met,   170
Since Merlin² paid his Demon all the monstrous debt.

XX.

"It shall be as thou wishest," said the Dame:
"All cates and dainties shall be stored there
Quickly on this feast-night: by the tambour frame
Her own lute thou wilt see: no time to spare,   175
For I am slow and feeble, and scarce dare
On such a catering trust my dizzy head.
Wait here, my child, with patience; kneel in prayer
The while: Ah! thou must needs the lady wed,
Or may I never leave my grave among the dead."   180

---

² st. xix, l. 9 *Merlin:* Can it have been that a confused recollection of the tale how Uther, transformed by Merlin into the likeness of Gorlois, loved Igerna in Tintagel, by night, was in the poet's mind?

XXI.

So saying, she hobbled off with busy fear.
The lover's endless minutes slowly pass'd;
The dame return'd, and whisper'd in his ear
To follow her; with aged eyes aghast
From fright of dim espial. Safe at last,   185
Through many a dusky gallery, they gain
The maiden's chamber, silken, hush'd, and chaste;
Where Porphyro took covert, pleas'd amain.
His poor guide hurried back with agues in her brain.

XXII.

Her falt'ring hand upon the balustrade,   190
Old Angela was feeling for the stair,
When Madeline, St. Agnes' charmed maid,
Rose, like a mission'd spirit, unaware:
With silver taper's light, and pious care,
She turn'd, and down the aged gossip led   195
To a safe level matting. Now prepare,
Young Porphyro, for gazing on that bed;
She comes, she comes again, like ring-dove fray'd and fled.

XXIII.

Out went the taper as she hurried in;
Its little smoke, in pallid moonshine, died: 200
She clos'd the door, she panted, all akin
To spirits of the air, and visions wide:
No uttered syllable, or, woe betide!
But to her heart, her heart was voluble,
Paining with eloquence her balmy side;   205
As though a tongueless nightingale should swell
Her throat in vain, and die, heart-stifled, in her dell.

XXIV.

A casement high and triple-arch'd there was,
All garlanded with carven imag'ries
Of fruits, and flowers, and bunches of knot-grass,   210
And diamonded with panes of quaint device,
Innumerable of stains and splendid dyes,
As are the tiger-moth's deep-damask'd wings;
And in the midst, 'mong thousand heraldries,
And twilight saints, and dim emblazonings,   215
A shielded scutcheon blush'd with blood of queens and kings.

XXV.

Full on this casement shone the wintry moon,
And threw warm gules³ on Madeline's fair breast,
As down she knelt for heaven's grace and boon;
Rose-bloom fell on her hands, together prest,   220
And on her silver cross soft amethyst,
And on her hair a glory, like a saint:
She seem'd a splendid angel, newly drest,
Save wings, for heaven:—Porphyro grew faint:
She knelt, so pure a thing, so free from mortal taint.   225

XXVI.

Anon his heart revives: her vespers done,
Of all its wreathed pearls her hair she frees;
Unclasps her warmed jewels one by one;
Loosens her fragrant boddice; by degrees
Her rich attire creeps rustling to her knees: 230
Half-hidden, like a mermaid in sea-weed,
Pensive awhile she dreams awake, and sees,

---

³ st. xxv, l. 2 *gules:* a heraldic term for *red:*—transmitted here through the coat-of-arms in the casement.

In fancy, fair St. Agnes in her bed,
But dares not look behind, or all the charm is fled.

XXVII.

Soon, trembling in her soft and chilly nest,   235
In sort of wakeful swoon, perplex'd she lay,
Until the poppied warmth of sleep oppress'd
Her soothed limbs, and soul fatigued away;
Flown, like a thought, until the morrow-day;
Blissfully haven'd both from joy and pain;   240
Clasp'd like a missal where swart Paynims pray;
Blinded alike from sunshine and from rain,
As though a rose should shut, and be a bud again.

XXVIII.

Stol'n to this paradise, and so entranced,
Porphyro gazed upon her empty dress,   245
And listen'd to her breathing, if it chanced
To wake into a slumberous tenderness;
Which when he heard, that minute did he bless,
And breath'd himself: then from the closet crept,
Noiseless as fear in a wide wilderness,   250
And over the hush'd carpet, silent, stept,
And 'tween the curtains peep'd, where, lo!—how fast she slept.

XXIX.

Then by the bed-side, where the faded moon
Made a dim, silver twilight, soft he set
A table, and, half anguish'd, threw thereon   255
A cloth of woven crimson, gold, and jet:—
O for some drowsy Morphean amulet!
The boisterous, midnight, festive clarion,
The kettle-drum, and far-heard clarionet,

Affray his ears, though but in dying tone:—   260
The hall door shuts again, and all the noise is gone.

XXX.

And still she slept an azure-lidded sleep,
In blanched linen, smooth, and lavender'd,
While he from forth the closet brought a heap
Of candied apple, quince, and plum, and gourd;   265
With jellies soother[4] than the creamy curd,
And lucent syrops, tinct with cinnamon;
Manna and dates, in argosy transferr'd
From Fez; and spiced dainties, every one,
From silken Samarcand to cedar'd Lebanon.   270

XXXI.

These delicates he heap'd with glowing hand
On golden dishes and in baskets bright
Of wreathed silver: sumptuous they stand
In the retired quiet of the night,
Filling the chilly room with perfume light.—   275
"And now, my love, my seraph fair, awake!
Thou art my heaven, and I thine eremite:
Open thine eyes, for meek St. Agnes' sake,
Or I shall drowse beside thee, so my soul doth ache."

XXXII.

Thus whispering, his warm, unnerved arm   280
Sank in her pillow. Shaded was her dream
By the dusk curtains:—'twas a midnight charm
Impossible to melt as iced stream:
The lustrous salvers in the moonlight gleam;
Broad golden fringe upon the carpet lies: 285

---

[4] st. xxx, l. 5 *soother:* seems used for *sweeter,* or *softer.*

It seem'd he never, never could redeem
From such a stedfast spell his lady's eyes;
So mus'd awhile, entoil'd in woofed phantasies.

XXXIII.

Awakening up, he took her hollow lute,—
Tumultuous,—and, in chords that tenderest be,   290
He play'd an ancient ditty, long since mute,
In Provence call'd, "La belle dame sans mercy:"
Close to her ear touching the melody;—
Wherewith disturb'd, she utter'd a soft moan:
He ceased—she panted quick—and suddenly   295
Her blue affrayed eyes wide open shone:
Upon his knees he sank, pale as smooth-sculptured stone.

XXXIV.

Her eyes were open, but she still beheld,
Now wide awake, the vision of her sleep:
There was a painful change, that nigh expell'd   300
The blisses of her dream so pure and deep
At which fair Madeline began to weep,
And moan forth witless words with many a sigh;
While still her gaze on Porphyro would keep;
Who knelt, with joined hands and piteous eye,   305
Fearing to move or speak, she look'd so dreamingly.

XXXV.

"Ah, Porphyro!" said she, "but even now
Thy voice was at sweet tremble in mine ear,
Made tuneable with every sweetest vow;
And those sad eyes were spiritual and clear: 310
How chang'd thou art! how pallid, chill, and drear!
Give me that voice again, my Porphyro,

Those looks immortal, those complainings dear!
Oh leave me not in this eternal woe,
For if thou diest, my Love, I know not where to go."   315

XXXVI.

Beyond a mortal man impassion'd far
At these voluptuous accents, he arose,
Ethereal, flush'd, and like a throbbing star
Seen mid the sapphire heaven's deep repose;
Into her dream he melted, as the rose   320
Blendeth its odour with the violet,—
Solution sweet: meantime the frost-wind blows
Like Love's alarum pattering the sharp sleet
Against the window-panes; St. Agnes' moon hath set.

XXXVII.

'Tis dark: quick pattereth the flaw-blown sleet:[5]   325
"This is no dream, my bride, my Madeline!"
'Tis dark: the iced gusts still rave and beat:
"No dream, alas! alas! and woe is mine!
Porphyro will leave me here to fade and pine.—
Cruel! what traitor could thee hither bring?   330
I curse not, for my heart is lost in thine,
Though thou forsakest a deceived thing;—
A dove forlorn and lost with sick unpruned wing."

XXXVIII.

"My Madeline! sweet dreamer! lovely bride!
Say, may I be for aye thy vassal blest?   335
Thy beauty's shield, heart-shap'd and vermeil dyed?
Ah, silver shrine, here will I take my rest
After so many hours of toil and quest,

---

[5] st. xxxvii, l. 1 *flaw:* flying blast.

A famish'd pilgrim,—saved by miracle.
Though I have found, I will not rob thy nest   340
Saving of thy sweet self; if thou think'st well
To trust, fair Madeline, to no rude infidel."

XXXIX.

'Hark! 'tis an elfin-storm from faery land,
Of haggard seeming, but a boon indeed:
Arise—arise! the morning is at hand;—   345
The bloated wassaillers will never heed:—
Let us away, my love, with happy speed;
There are no ears to hear, or eyes to see,—
Drown'd all in Rhenish and the sleepy mead:
Awake! arise! my love, and fearless be,   350
For o'er the southern moors I have a home for thee."

XL.

She hurried at his words, beset with fears,
For there were sleeping dragons all around,
At glaring watch, perhaps, with ready spears—
Down the wide stairs a darkling way they found.—   355
In all the house was heard no human sound.
A chain-droop'd lamp was flickering by each door;
The arras, rich with horseman, hawk, and hound,
Flutter'd in the besieging wind's uproar;
And the long carpets rose along the gusty floor.   360

XLI.

They glide, like phantoms, into the wide hall;
Like phantoms, to the iron porch, they glide;
Where lay the Porter, in uneasy sprawl,
With a huge empty flaggon by his side;
The wakeful bloodhound rose, and shook his hide,   365

But his sagacious eye an inmate owns:
By one, and one, the bolts full easy slide:—
The chains lie silent on the footworn stones;—
The key turns, and the door upon its hinges groan.

XLII.

And they are gone: ay, ages long ago   370
These lovers fled away into the storm.
That night the Baron dreamt of many a woe,
And all his warrior-guests, with shade and form
Of witch, and demon, and large coffin-worm,
Were long be-nightmar'd. Angela the old   375
Died palsy-twitch'd, with meagre face deform;
The Beadsman, after thousand aves told,
For aye unsought for slept among his ashes cold.

Hyperion:

a fragment

INTRODUCTION

BEGUN in Dec. 1818: in hand during the next autumn: dropped Sep. 1819.

This famous fragmentary poem seems to have afforded Keats less satisfaction than any other of his works. It was printed, as the "Advertisement" shows, at his Publishers' desire, "and contrary to the wish of the author." Still later, he "re-cast it into the shape of a Vision, which remains equally unfinished." "I have given up *Hyperion,*" Keats writes from Winchester, Sep. 22, 1819 "—there were too many Miltonic inversions in it—Miltonic verse cannot be written but in an artful, or rather, artist's humour. I wish to give myself up to other sensations. English ought to be kept up." This phrase apparently refers to the mood in which he had just written those noble lines to *Autumn,* which I put, with *Lamia,* and five or six more pieces, amongst his maturest work; the work wherein art touches its genuine triumph in concealing itself: the work which, in matter and manner alike, embodies his most essential, his most intimate, genius. And, in the remarks which follow, the poet clearly shows a consciousness that in *Hyperion* the "artist's humour "was too prevalent: "the false beauty, proceeding from art," blended with "the true voice of feeling."— Keats, criticizing here for the last time his own work, touches on the note which is most sensible in his poetry, as it is that which lay the deepest in his own nature. Almost more than passion for beauty,— although, indeed it is, rather, itself the fine flower of beauty,— tenderness,—almost passing into tremulousness,—seems to me his characteristic. Here and there, whilst he was little more than a boy, we hear this note in excess. But Keats, in both the qualities just named, true child of Spenser, has also the manliness of nature, the sanity of sentiment, which underlie everywhere that river of gold which ripples through the *Faerie Queene.* Beyond any of his great compeers during the last two centuries, (if I may here venture thus to sum up the imperfect criticisms on his genius which are offered in these notes), Keats had inherited, not only as Man but as Poet,—or rather, as Poet because he was so as Man,—the inspiration and the magnanimity of

the great age of our Muses;—more than any, he is true English-
Elizabethan:—Had the years of Milton been destined for him, of him,
more than of any other it might have been prophesied,

Fortunate puer! Tu nunc eris alter ab illo.

Despite the marvellous grandeur of its execution, the judgment of
Keats upon this work appears to be thoroughly well founded. After an
introduction worthy to be compared with what the Propylaea of the
Acropolis at Athens must have been, at once in severe majesty and in
refinement of execution, the interest of the story rapidly and
irremediably falls off. It is, truly, to take a phrase from the Preface to
Endymion, "too late a day." The attempt to revivify an ancient myth,—
as distinguished from an ancient story of human life,—however
alluring, however illustrated by poets of genius, seems to me
essentially impossible. It is for the details, not for the whole, that we
read *Hyperion,* or *Prometheus Unbound,* or the German *Iphigeneia.*
Like the great majority of post-classical verse in classical languages,
those modern myths are but exercises, (and, as such, with their value
to the writer), on a splendid scale. The story of which *Hyperion* tells
the beginning is, in fact, far too remote, too alien from the modern
world: it has neither any definite symbolical meaning, nor any of that
"soft humanity" which underlies the wild magic of *Lamia,* and has
rendered possible a picture, true not only to Corinth two thousand
years ago, but to all time.—Yet, with such strange vital force has he
penetrated into the Titan world, and all but given the reality of life to
the old shadows before him, that, had this miracle been possible, we
may fairly say that Keats would have worked it.

The author was, hence, right in "giving up" *Hyperion.* Yet, by a
singular irony of literary fate, *Hyperion* was the first of his poems
which seems to have reached fame beyond his own English circle of
admirers. Byron, in a passage often quoted, placed its sublimity on a
level with Aeschylus. But the criticisms which it called forth from
Shelley are the most noteworthy. In Nov. 1820 we find him writing
that he has received " a volume of poems by Keats; in other respects
insignificant enough, but containing the fragment of a poem called
Hyperion.... It is certainly an astonishing piece of writing." Nor was
this Shelley's first impression only; for on 15 Feb. 1821 he returns to
Keats: "His other poems are worth little; but, if the *Hyperion* be not
grand poetry, none has been produced by our contemporaries."—If we
remember the masterpieces contained in the precious little book of

1820, it may be reasonably held that even the political antagonists of Keats and his friends could hardly have exceeded these criticisms in blind prosaic injustice. So may one great poet,—and he, snow-pure from taint of envy or malice,—misunderstand and misestimate another!

My object in these notes has been only to aid readers to enjoy the Poems before them; not to offer a formal estimate of the genius of Keats, or of his place in English poetry. But, as the writer is little known in England, I will suggest to some readers that in André Chénier (1762–1704) they will find a poet curiously and, on the whole, (I would venture to think), nearly analogous to Keats. In both, Beauty is the first and last note heard; both were led to the legends of Hellas as a natural source of inspiration; in both, freshness of phrase, picturesqueness of form and presentation, easy abundance of imaginative description, are conspicuous. I may refer, as illustrations, to Chénier's Epistle to Le Brun and the Marquis of Brazais (No. i, Ed. 1852), to the Third Epistle to Le Brun, and that to De Pange (No. iv): to the fragmentary Idyll, *Les Colombes* (No. xix), and that numbered xii, the influence of which over Alfred de Musset is obvious.— Chénier's longer Idylls, though brilliant in skill, have too much of Gallic epigram and rhetoric to do full justice to his exquisite genius.

Hyperion
BOOK I

DEEP in the shady sadness of a vale
Far sunken from the healthy breath of morn,
Far from the fiery noon, and eve's one star,
Sat gray-hair'd Saturn, quiet as a stone,
Still as the silence round about his lair;   5
Forest on forest hung about his head
Like cloud on cloud. No stir of air was there,
Not so much life as on a summer's day
Robs not one light seed from the feather'd grass,
But where the dead leaf fell, there did it rest.   10
A stream went voiceless by, still deadened more
By reason of his fallen divinity
Spreading a shade: the Naiad 'mid her reeds
Press'd her cold finger closer to her lips.

Along the margin-sand large foot-marks went,   15
No further than to where his feet had stray'd,
And slept there since. Upon the sodden ground
His old right hand lay nerveless, listless, dead,
Unsceptred; and his realmless eyes were closed;
While his bow'd head seem'd list'ning to the Earth,   20
His ancient mother, for some comfort yet.

It seem'd no force could wake him from his place;
But there came one, who with a kindred hand
Touch'd his wide shoulders, after bending low
With reverence, though to one who knew it not.   25
She was a Goddess of the infant world;

By her in stature the tall Amazon
Had stood a pigmy's height: she would have ta'en
Achilles by the hair and bent his neck;
Or with a finger stay'd Ixion's wheel.   30
Her face was large as that of Memphian sphinx,
Pedestal'd haply in a palace court,
When sages look'd to Egypt for their lore.
But oh! how unlike marble was that face:
How beautiful, if sorrow had not made   35
Sorrow more beautiful than Beauty's self.
There was a listening fear in her regard,
As if calamity had but begun;
As if the vanward clouds of evil days
Had spent their malice, and the sullen rear   40
Was with its stored thunder labouring up.
One hand she press'd upon that aching spot
Where beats the human heart, as if just there,
Though an immortal, she felt cruel pain:
The other upon Saturn's bended neck   45
She laid, and to the level of his ear
Leaning with parted lips, some words she spake
In solemn tenour and deep organ tone:
Some mourning words, which in our feeble tongue
Would come in these like accents; O how frail   50
To that large utterance of the early Gods!
"Saturn, look up!—though wherefore, poor old King?
I have no comfort for thee, no not one:
I cannot say, "O wherefore sleepest thou?'
For heaven is parted from thee, and the earth   55
Knows thee not, thus afflicted, for a God;
And ocean too, with all its solemn noise,
Has from thy sceptre pass'd; and all the air
Is emptied of thine hoary majesty.
Thy thunder, conscious of the new command,   60

Rumbles reluctant o'er our fallen house;
And thy sharp lightning in unpractised hands
Scorches and burns our once serene domain.
O aching time! O moments big as years!
All as ye pass swell out the monstrous truth,   65
And press it so upon our weary griefs
That unbelief has not a space to breathe.
Saturn, sleep on:—O thoughtless, why did I
Thus violate thy slumbrous solitude?
Why should I ope thy melancholy eyes?   70
Saturn, sleep on! while at thy feet I weep."

   As when, upon a tranced summer-night,
Those green-rob'd senators of mighty woods,
Tall oaks, branch-charmed by the earnest stars,
Dream, and so dream all night without a stir,   75
Save from one gradual solitary gust
Which comes upon the silence, and dies off,
As if the ebbing air had but one wave;
So came these words and went; the while in tears
She touch'd her fair large forehead to the ground,   80
Just where her falling hair might be outspread
A soft and silken mat for Saturn's feet.
One moon, with alteration slow, had shed
Her silver seasons four upon the night,
And still these two were postured motionless,   85
Like natural sculpture in cathedral cavern;
The frozen God still couchant on the earth,
And the sad Goddess weeping at his feet:
Until at length old Saturn lifted up
His faded eyes, and saw his kingdom gone,   90
And all the gloom and sorrow of the place,
And that fair kneeling Goddess; and then spake,
As with a palsied tongue, and while his beard

Shook horrid with such aspen-malady:
"O tender spouse of gold Hyperion, 95
Thea, I feel thee ere I see thy face;
Look up, and let me see our doom in it;
Look up, and tell me if this feeble shape
Is Saturn's; tell me, if thou hear'st the voice
Of Saturn; tell me, if this wrinkling brow, 100
Naked and bare of its great diadem,
Peers like the front of Saturn. Who had power
To make me desolate? whence came the strength?
How was it nurtur'd to such bursting forth,
While Fate seem'd strangled in my nervous grasp? 105
But it is so; and I am smother'd up,
And buried from all godlike exercise
Of influence benign on planets pale,
Of admonitions to the winds and seas,
Of peaceful sway above man's harvesting, 110
And all those acts which Deity supreme
Doth ease its heart of love in.—I am gone
Away from my own bosom: I have left
My strong identity, my real self,
Somewhere between the throne, and where I sit 115
Here on this spot of earth. Search, Thea, search!
Open thine eyes eterne, and sphere them round
Upon all space: space starr'd, and lorn of light;
Space region'd with life-air; and barren void;
Spaces of fire, and all the yawn of hell.— 120
Search, Thea, search! and tell me, if thou seest
A certain shape or shadow, making way
With wings or chariot fierce to repossess
A heaven he lost erewhile: it must—it must
Be of ripe progress—Saturn must be King. 125
Yes, there must be a golden victory;
There must be Gods thrown down, and trumpets blown

Of triumph calm, and hymns of festival
Upon the gold clouds metropolitan,
Voices of soft proclaim, and silver stir   130
Of strings in hollow shells; and there shall be
Beautiful things made new, for the surprise
Of the sky-children; I will give command:
Thea! Thea! Thea! where is Saturn?"

   This passion lifted him upon his feet,   135
And made his hands to struggle in the air,
His Druid locks to shake and ooze with sweat,
His eyes to fever out, his voice to cease.
He stood, and heard not Thea's sobbing deep;
A little time, and then again he snatch'd   140
Utterance thus.—"But cannot I create?
Cannot I form? Cannot I fashion forth
Another world, another universe,
To overbear and crumble this to nought?
Where is another chaos? Where?"—That word   145
Found way unto Olympus, and made quake
The rebel three.—Thea was startled up,
And in her bearing was a sort of hope,
As thus she quick-voic'd spake, yet full of awe.

   "This cheers our fallen house: come to our friends,   150
O Saturn! come away, and give them heart;
I know the covert, for thence came I hither."
Thus brief; then with beseeching eyes she went
With backward footing through the shade a space:
He follow'd, and she turn'd to lead the way   155
Through aged boughs, that yielded like the mist
Which eagles cleave upmounting from their nest.

Meanwhile in other realms big tears were shed,
More sorrow like to this, and such like woe,
Too huge for mortal tongue or pen of scribe: 160
The Titans fierce, self hid, or prison-bound,
Groan'd for the old allegiance once more,
And listen'd in sharp pain for Saturn's voice.
But one of the whole mammoth-brood still kept
His sov'reignty, and rule, and majesty;—   165
Blazing Hyperion on his orbed fire
Still sat, still snuff'd the incense, teeming up
From man to the sun's God; yet unsecure:
For as among us mortals omens drear
Fright and perplex, so also shuddered he—   170
Not at dog's howl, or gloom-bird's hated screech,
Or the familiar visiting of one
Upon the first toll of his passing-bell,
Or prophesyings of the midnight lamp;
But horrors, portion'd to a giant nerve,   175
Oft made Hyperion ache. His palace bright
Bastion'd with pyramids of glowing gold,
And touch'd with shade of bronzed obelisks,
Glar'd a blood-red through all its thousand courts,
Arches, and domes, and fiery galleries;   180
And all its curtains of Aurorian clouds
Flush'd angerly: while sometimes eagle's wings,
Unseen before by Gods or wondering men,
Darken'd the place; and neighing steeds were heard,
Not heard before by Gods or wondering men.   185
Also, when he would taste the spicy wreaths
Of incense, breath'd aloft from sacred hills,
Instead of sweets, his ample palate took
Savour of poisonous brass and metal sick:
And so, when harbour'd in the sleepy west,   190
After the full completion of fair day,—

222

For rest divine upon exalted couch
And slumber in the arms of melody,
He pac'd away the pleasant hours of ease
With stride colossal, on from hall to hall;   195
While far within each aisle and deep recess,
His winged minions in close clusters stood,
Amaz'd and full of fear; like anxious men
Who on wide plains gather in panting troops,
When earthquakes jar their battlements and towers.   200
Even now, while Saturn, rous'd from icy trance,
Went step for step with Thea through the woods,
Hyperion, leaving twilight in the rear,
Came slope upon the threshold of the west;
Then, as was wont, his palace-door flew ope   205
In smoothest silence, save what solemn tubes,
Blown by the serious Zephyrs, gave of sweet
And wandering sounds, slow-breathed melodies;
And like a rose in vermeil tint and shape,
In fragrance soft, and coolness to the eye,   210
That inlet to severe magnificence
Stood full blown, for the God to enter in.

He enter'd, but he enter'd full of wrath;
His flaming robes stream'd out beyond his heels,
And gave a roar, as if of earthly fire,   215
That scar'd away the meek ethereal Hours
And made their dove-wings tremble. On he flared,
From stately nave to nave, from vault to vault,
Through bowers of fragrant and enwreathed light,
And diamond-paved lustrous long arcades,   220
Until he reach'd the great main cupola;
There standing fierce beneath, he stampt his foot,
And from the basements deep to the high towers
Jarr'd his own golden region; and before

The quavering thunder thereupon had ceas'd,   225
His voice leapt out, despite of godlike curb,
To this result: "O dreams of day and night!
O monstrous forms! O effigies of pain!
O spectres busy in a cold, cold gloom!
O lank-ear'd Phantoms of black-weeded pools!   230
Why do I know ye? why have I seen ye? why
Is my eternal essence thus distraught
To see and to behold these horrors new?
Saturn is fallen, am I too to fall?
Am I to leave this haven of my rest,   235
This cradle of my glory, this soft clime,
This calm luxuriance of blissful light,
These crystalline pavilions, aud pure fanes,
Of all my lucent empire? It is left
Deserted, void, nor any haunt of mine.   240
The blaze, the splendor, and the symmetry,
I cannot see—but darkness, death and darkness.
Even here, into my centre of repose,
The shady visions come to domineer,
Insult, and blind, and stifle up my pomp.—   245
Fall!—No, by Tellus and her briny robes!
Over the fiery frontier of my realms
I will advance a terrible right arm
Shall scare that infant thunderer, rebel Jove,
And bid old Saturn take his throne again."—   250
He spake, and ceas'd, the while a heavier threat
Held struggle with his throat but came not forth;
For as in theatres of crowded men
Hubbub increases more they call out "Hush!"
So at Hyperion's words the Phantoms pale   255
Bestirr'd themselves, thrice horrible and cold;
And from the mirror'd level where he stood
A mist arose, as from a scummy marsh.

At this, through all his bulk an agony
Crept gradual, from the feet unto the crown,   260
Like a lithe serpent vast and muscular
Making slow way, with head and neck convuls'd
From over-strained might. Releas'd, he fled
To the eastern gates, and full six dewy hours
Before the dawn in season due should blush,   265
He breath'd fierce breath against the sleepy portals,
Clear'd them of heavy vapours, burst them wide
Suddenly on the ocean's chilly streams.
The planet orb of fire, whereon he rode
Each day from east to west the heavens through,   270
Spun round in sable curtaining of clouds;
Not therefore veiled quite, blindfold, and hid,
But ever and anon the glancing spheres,
Circles, and arcs, and broad-belting colure,
Glow'd through, and wrought upon the muffling dark   275
Sweet-shaped lightnings from the nadir deep
Up to the zenith,—hieroglyphics old,
Which sages and keen-eyed astrologers
Then living on the earth, with labouring thought
Won from the gaze of many centuries: 280
Now lost, save what we find on remnants huge
Of stone, or marble swart; their import gone,
Their wisdom long since fled.—Two wings this orb
Possess'd for glory, two fair argent wings,
Ever exalted at the God's approach: 285
And now, from forth the gloom their plumes immense
Rose, one by one, till all outspreaded were;
While still the dazzling globe maintain'd eclipse,
Awaiting for Hyperion's command.
Fain would he have commanded, fain took throne   290
And bid the day begin, if but for change.
He might not:—No, though a primeval God:

The sacred seasons might not be disturb'd.
Therefore the operations of the dawn
Stay'd in their birth, even as here 'tis told.   295
Those silver wings expanded sisterly,
Eager to sail their orb; the porches wide
Open'd upon the dusk demesnes of night;
And the bright Titan, phrenzied with new woes,
Unus'd to bend, by hard compulsion bent   300
His spirit to the sorrow of the time;
And all along a dismal rack of clouds,
Upon the boundaries of day and night,
He stretch'd himself in grief and radiance faint.
There as he lay, the Heaven with its stars   305
Look'd down on him with pity, and the voice
Of Coelus, from the universal space,
Thus whisper'd low and solemn in his ear.
"O brightest of my children dear, earth-born
And sky-engendered, Son of Mysteries   310
All unrevealed even to the powers
Which met at thy creating; at whose joys
And palpitations sweet, and pleasures soft,
I, Coelus, wonder, how they came and whence;
And at the fruits thereof what shapes they be,   315
Distinct, and visible; symbols divine,
Manifestations of that beauteous life
Diffus'd unseen throughout eternal space:
Of these new-form'd art thou, oh brightest child!
Of these, thy brethren and the Goddesses!   320
There is sad feud among ye, and rebellion
Of son against his sire. I saw him fall,
I saw my first-born tumbled from his throne!
To me his arms were spread, to me his voice
Found way from forth the thunders round his head!   325
Pale wox I, and in vapours hid my face.

Art thou, too, near such doom? vague fear there is:
For I have seen my sons most unlike Gods.
Divine ye were created, and divine
In sad demeanour, solemn, undisturb'd,   330
Unruffled, like high Gods, ye liv'd and ruled:
Now I behold in you fear, hope, and wrath;
Actions of rage and passion; even as
I see them, on the mortal world beneath,
In men who die.—This is the grief, O Son!   335
Sad sign of ruin, sudden dismay, and fall!
Yet do thou strive; as thou art capable,
As thou canst move about, an evident God;
And canst oppose to each malignant hour
Ethereal presence:—I am but a voice;   340
My life is but the life of winds and tides,
No more than winds and tides can I avail:—
But thou canst.—Be thou therefore in the van
Of circumstance; yea, seize the arrow's barb
Before the tense string murmur.—To the earth!   345
For there thou wilt find Saturn, and his woes.
Meantime I will keep watch on thy bright sun,
And of thy seasons be a careful nurse."—
Ere half this region-whisper had come down,
Hyperion arose, and on the stars   350
Lifted his curved lids, and kept them wide
Until it ceas'd; and still he kept them wide:
And still they were the same bright, patient stars.
Then with a slow incline of his broad breast,
Like to a diver in the pearly seas,   355
Forward he stoop'd over the airy shore,
And plung'd all noiseless into the deep night.

Hyperion

BOOK II

JUST at the self-same beat of Time's wide wings
Hyperion slid into the rustled air,
And Saturn gain'd with Thea that sad place
Where Cybele and the bruised Titans mourn'd.
It was a den where no insulting light   5
Could glimmer on their tears; where their own groans
They felt, but heard not, for the solid roar
Of thunderous waterfalls and torrents hoarse,
Pouring a constant bulk, uncertain where.
Crag jutting forth to crag, and rocks that seem'd   10
Ever as if just rising from a sleep,
Forehead to forehead held their monstrous horns;
And thus in thousand hugest phantasies
Made a fit roofing to this nest of woe.
Instead of thrones, hard flint they sat upon,   15
Couches of rugged stone, and slaty ridge
Stubborn'd with iron. All were not assembled:
Some chain'd in torture, and some wandering.
Coeus, and Gyges, and Briareüs,
Typhon, and Dolor, and Porphyrion,   20
With many more, the brawniest in assault,
Were pent in regions of laborious breath;
Dungeon'd in opaque element, to keep
Their clenched teeth still clench'd, and all their limbs
Lock'd up like veins of metal, crampt and screw'd;   25
Without a motion, save of their big hearts
Heaving in pain, and horribly convuls'd
With sanguine feverous boiling gurge of pulse.

Mnemosyne was straying in the world;
Far from her moon had Phoebe wandered;   30
And many else were free to roam abroad,
But for the main, here found they covert drear.
Scarce images of life, one here, one there,
Lay vast and edgeways; like a dismal cirque
Of Druid stones, upon a forlorn moor,   35
When the chill rain begins at shut of eve,
In dull November, and their chancel vault,
The Heaven itself, is blinded throughout night.
Each one kept shroud, nor to his neighbour gave
Or word, or look, or action of despair.   40
Creus was one; his ponderous iron mace
Lay by him, and a shatter'd rib of rock
Told of his rage, ere he thus sank and pined.
Iapetus another; in his grasp,
A serpent's plashy neck; its barbed tongue   45
Squeez'd from the gorge, and all its uncurl'd length
Dead; and because the creature could not spit
Its poison in the eyes of conquering Jove.
Next Cottus: prone he lay, chin uppermost,
As though in pain; for still upon the flint   50
He ground severe his skull, with open mouth
And eyes at horrid working. Nearest him
Asia, born of most enormous Caf,
Who cost her mother Tellus keener pangs,
Though feminine, than any of her sons: 55
More thought than woe was in her dusky face,
For she was prophesying of her glory;
And in her wide imagination stood
Palm-shaded temples, and high rival fanes,
By Oxus or in Ganges' sacred isles.   60
Even as Hope upon her anchor leans,
So leant she, not so fair, upon a tusk

Shed from the broadest of her elephants.
Above her, on a crag's uneasy shelve,
Upon his elbow rais'd, all prostrate else,   65
Shadow'd Enceladus; once tame and mild
As grazing ox unworried in the meads;
Now tiger-passion'd, lion-thoughted, wroth,
He meditated, plotted, and even now
Was hurling mountains in that second war,   70
Not long delay'd, that scar'd the younger Gods
To hide themselves in forms of beast and bird.
Nor far hence Atlas; and beside him prone
Phorcus, the sire of Gorgons. Neighbour'd close
Oceanus, and Tethys, in whose lap   75
Sobb'd Clymene among her tangled hair.
In midst of all lay Themis, at the feet
Of Ops the queen all clouded round from sight;
No shape distinguishable, more than when
Thick night confounds the pine-tops with the clouds: 80
And many else whose names may not be told.
For when the Muse's wings are air-ward spread,
Who shall delay her flight? And she must chaunt
Of Saturn, and his guide, who now had climb'd
With damp and slippery footing from a depth   85
More horrid still. Above a sombre cliff
Their heads appear'd, and up their stature grew
Till on the level height their steps found ease:
Then Thea spread abroad her trembling arms
Upon the precincts of this nest of pain,   90
And sidelong fix'd her eye on Saturn's face:
There saw she direst strife; the supreme God
At war with all the frailty of grief,
Of rage, of fear, anxiety, revenge,
Remorse, spleen, hope, but most of all despair.   95
Against these plagues he strove in vain; for Fate

Had pour'd a mortal oil upon his head,
A disanointing poison: so that Thea,
Affrighted, kept her still, and let him pass
First onwards in, among the fallen tribe.   100

   As with us mortal men, the laden heart
Is persecuted more, and fever'd more,
When it is nighing to the mournful house
Where other hearts are sick of the same bruise;
So Saturn, as he walk'd into the midst,   105
Felt faint, and would have sunk among the rest,
But that he met Enceladus's eye,
Whose mightiness, and awe of him, at once
Came like an inspiration; and he shouted,
"Titans, behold your God!" at which some groan'd;   110
Some started on their feet; some also shouted;
Some wept, some wail'd, all bow'd with reverence;
And Ops, uplifting her black folded veil,
Show'd her pale cheeks, and all her forehead wan,
Her eye-brows thin and jet, and hollow eyes.   115
There is a roaring in the bleak-grown pines
When Winter lifts his voice; there is a noise
Among immortals when a God gives sign,
With hushing finger, how he means to load
His tongue with the full weight of utterless thought,   120
With thunder, and with music, and with pomp:
Such noise is like the roar of bleak-grown pines;
Which, when it ceases in this mountain'd world,
No other sound succeeds; but ceasing here,
Among these fallen, Saturn's voice therefrom   125
Grew up like organ, that begins anew
Its strain, when other harmonies, stopt short,
Leave the dinn'd air vibrating silverly.
Thus grew it up—"Not in my own sad breast,

Which is its own great judge and searcher out,   130
Can I find reason why ye should be thus:
Not in the legends of the first of days,
Studied from that old spirit-leaved book
Which starry Uranus with finger bright
Sav'd from the shores of darkness, when the waves   135
Low-ebb'd still hid it up in shallow gloom;—
And the which book ye know I ever kept
For my firm-based footstool:—Ah, infirm!
Not there, nor in sign, symbol, or portent
Of element, earth, water, air, and fire,—   140
At war, at peace, or inter-quarreling
One against one, or two, or three, or all
Each several one against the other three,
As fire with air loud warring when rain-floods
Drown both, and press them both against earth's face,   145
Where, finding sulphur, a quadruple wrath
Unhinges the poor world;—not in that strife,
Wherefrom I take strange lore, and read it deep,
Can I find reason why ye should be thus:
No, no-where can unriddle, though I search,   150
And pore on Nature's universal scroll
Even to swooning, why ye, Divinities,
The first-born of all shap'd and palpable Gods,
Should cower beneath what, in comparison,
Is untremendous might. Yet ye are here,   155
O'erwhelm'd, and spurn'd, and batter'd, ye are here!
O Titans, shall I say 'Arise!'—Ye groan:
Shall I say 'Crouch!'—Ye groan. What can I then?
O Heaven wide! O unseen parent dear!
What can I? Tell me, all ye brethren Gods,   160
How we can war, how engine our great wrath!
O speak your counsel now, for Saturn's ear
Is all a-hunger'd. Thou, Oceanus,

Ponderest high and deep; and in thy face
I see, astonied, that severe content   165
Which comes of thought and musing: give us help!"

    So ended Saturn; and the God of the Sea,
Sophist and sage, from no Athenian grove,
But cogitation in his watery shades,
Arose, with locks not oozy, and began,   170
In murmurs, which his first-endeavouring tongue
Caught infant-like from the far-foamed sands.
"O ye, whom wrath consumes! who, passion-stung,[1]
Writhe at defeat, and nurse your agonies!
Shut up your senses, stifle up your ears,   175
My voice is not a bellows unto ire.
Yet listen, ye who will, whilst I bring proof
How ye, perforce, must be content to stoop:
And in the proof much comfort will I give,
If ye will take that comfort in its truth.   180
We fall by course of Nature's law, not force
Of thunder, or of Jove. Great Saturn, thou
Hast sifted well the atom-universe;
But for this reason, that thou art the King,
And only blind from sheer supremacy,   185
One avenue was shaded from thine eyes,
Through which I wandered to eternal truth.
And first, as thou wast not the first of powers,
So art thou not the last; it cannot be:
Thou art not the beginning nor the end.   190
From chaos and parental darkness came
Light, the first fruits of that intestine broil,

---

[1] l. 173 - 243 The speech of Oceanus, with its reasonings from natural law and development, may remind us of the rationalistic vein which we find, here and there, throughout the *Idylls of the King.*

That sullen ferment, which for wondrous ends
Was ripening in itself. The ripe hour came,
And with it light, and light, engendering   195
Upon its own producer, forthwith touch'd
The whole enormous matter into life.
Upon that very hour, our parentage,
The Heavens and the Earth, were manifest:
Then thou first-born, and we the giant-race,   200
Found ourselves ruling new and beauteous realms.
Now comes the pain of truth, to whom 'tis pain;
O folly! for to bear all naked truths,
And to envisage circumstance, all calm,
That is the top of sovereignty. Mark well!   205
As Heaven and Earth are fairer, fairer far
Than Chaos and blank Darkness, though once chiefs;
And as we show beyond that Heaven and Earth
In form and shape compact and beautiful,
In will, in action free, companionship,   210
And thousand other signs of purer life;
So on our heels a fresh perfection treads,
A power more strong in beauty, born of us
And fated to excel us, as we pass
In glory that old Darkness: nor are we   215
Thereby more conquer'd, than by us the rule
Of shapeless Chaos. Say, doth the dull soil
Quarrel with the proud forests it hath fed,
And feedeth still, more comely than itself?
Can it deny the chiefdom of green groves?   220
Or shall the tree be envious of the dove
Because it cooeth, and hath snowy wings
To wander wherewithal and find its joys?
We are such forest-trees, and our fair boughs
Have bred forth, not pale solitary doves,   225
But eagles golden-feather'd, who do tower

Above us in their beauty, and must reign
In right thereof; for 'tis the eternal law
That first in beauty should be first in might:
Yea, by that law, another race may drive   230
Our conquerors to mourn as we do now.
Have ye beheld the young God of the Seas,
My dispossessor? Have ye seen his face?
Have ye beheld his chariot, foam'd along
By noble winged creatures he hath made?   235
I saw him on the calmed waters scud,
With such a glow of beauty in his eyes,
That it enforc'd me to bid sad farewell
To all my empire: farewell sad I took,
And hither came, to see how dolorous fate   240
Had wrought upon ye; and how I might best
Give consolation in this woe extreme.
Receive the truth, and let it be your balm."

    Whether through poz'd conviction, or disdain,
They guarded silence, when Oceanus   245
Left murmuring, what deepest thought can tell?
But so it was, none answer'd for a space,
Save one whom none regarded, Clymene;
And yet she answer'd not, only complain'd,
With hectic lips, and eyes up-looking mild,   250
Thus wording timidly among the fierce:
"O Father, I am here the simplest voice,
And all my knowledge is that joy is gone,
And this thing woe crept in among our hearts,
There to remain for ever, as I fear: 255
I would not bode of evil, if I thought
So weak a creature could turn off the help
Which by just right should come of mighty Gods;
Yet let me tell my sorrow, let me tell

Of what I heard, and how it made me weep,   260
And know that we had parted from all hope.
I stood upon a shore, a pleasant shore,
Where a sweet clime was breathed from a land
Of fragrance, quietness, and trees, and flowers.
Full of calm joy it was, as I of grief;   265
Too full of joy and soft delicious warmth;
So that I felt a movement in my heart
To chide, and to reproach that solitude
With songs of misery, music of our woes;
And sat me down, and took a mouthed shell   270
And murmur'd into it, and made melody—
O melody no more! for while I sang,
And with poor skill let pass into the breeze
The dull shell's echo, from a bowery strand
Just opposite, an island of the sea,   275
There came enchantment with the shifting wind,
That did both drown and keep alive my ears.
I threw my shell away upon the sand,
And a wave fill'd it, as my sense was fill'd
With that new blissful golden melody.   280
A living death was in each gush of sounds,
Each family of rapturous hurried notes,
That fell, one after one, yet all at once,
Like pearl beads dropping sudden from their string:
And then another, then another strain,   285
Each like a dove leaving its olive perch,
With music wing'd instead of silent plumes,
To hover round my head, and make me sick
Of joy and grief at once. Grief overcame,
And I was stopping up my frantic ears,   290
When, past all hindrance of my trembling hands,
A voice came sweeter, sweeter than all tune,
And still it cried, 'Apollo! young Apollo!

'The morning-bright Apollo! young Apollo!'
I fled, it follow'd me, and cried 'Apollo!'   295
O Father, and O Brethren, had ye felt
Those pains of mine; O Saturn, hadst thou felt,
Ye would not call this too indulged tongue
Presumptuous, in thus venturing to be heard."

   So far her voice flow'd on, like timorous brook   300
That, lingering along a pebbled coast,
Doth fear to meet the sea: but sea it met,
And shudder'd; for the overwhelming voice
Of huge Enceladus swallow'd it in wrath:
The ponderous syllables, like sullen waves   305
In the half-glutted hollows of reef-rocks,
Came booming thus, while still upon his arm
He lean'd; not rising, from supreme contempt.
Or shall we listen to the over-wise,
Or to the over-foolish giant, Gods?   310
Not thunderbolt on thunderbolt, till all
That rebel Jove's whole armoury were spent,
Not world on world upon these shoulders piled,
Could agonize me more than baby-words
In midst of this dethronement horrible.   315
Speak! roar! shout! yell! ye sleepy Titans all.
Do ye forget the blows, the buffets vile?
Are ye not smitten by a youngling arm?
Dost thou forget, sham Monarch of the Waves,
Thy scalding in the seas? What, have I rous'd   320
Your spleens with so few simple words as these?
O joy! for now I see ye are not lost:
O joy! for now I see a thousand eyes
Wide glaring for revenge!—As this he said,
He lifted up his stature vast, and stood,   325
Still without intermission speaking thus:

"Now ye are flames, I'll tell you how to burn,
And purge the ether of our enemies;
How to feed fierce the crooked stings of fire,
And singe away the swollen clouds of Jove,   330
Stifling that puny essence in its tent.
O let him feel the evil he hath done;
For though I scorn Oceanus's lore,
Much pain have I for more than loss of realms:
The days of peace and slumberous calm are fled;   335
Those days, all innocent of scathing war,
When all the fair Existences of heaven
Came open-eyed to guess what we would speak:—
That was before our brows were taught to frown,
Before our lips knew else but solemn sounds;   340
That was before we knew the winged thing,
Victory, might be lost, or might be won.
And be ye mindful that Hyperion,
Our brightest brother, still is undisgraced—
Hyperion, lo! his radiance is here!"   345

    All eyes were on Enceladus's face,
And they beheld, while still Hyperion's name
Flew from his lips up to the vaulted rocks,
A pallid gleam across his features stern:
Not savage, for he saw full many a God   350
Wroth as himself. He look'd upon them all,
And in each face he saw a gleam of light,
But splendider in Saturn's, whose hoar locks
Shone like the bubbling foam about a keel
When the prow sweeps into a midnight cove.   355
In pale and silver silence they remain'd,
Till suddenly a splendour, like the morn,
Pervaded all the beetling gloomy steeps,
All the sad spaces of oblivion,

238

And every gulf, and every chasm old,   360
And every height, and every sullen depth,
Voiceless, or hoarse with loud tormented streams:
And all the everlasting cataracts,
And all the headlong torrents far and near,
Mantled before in darkness and huge shade,   365
Now saw the light and made it terrible.
It was Hyperion:—a granite peak
His bright feet touch'd, and there he stay'd to view
The misery his brilliance had betray'd
To the most hateful seeing of itself.   370
Golden his hair of short Numidian curl,
Regal his shape majestic, a vast shade
In midst of his own brightness, like the bulk
Of Memnon's image at the set of sun
To one who travels from the dusking East: 375
Sighs, too, as mournful as that Memnon's harp
He utter'd, while his hands contemplative
He press'd together, and in silence stood.
Despondence seiz'd again the fallen Gods
At sight of the dejected King of Day,   380
And many hid their faces from the light:
But fierce Enceladus sent forth his eyes
Among the brotherhood; and, at their glare,
Uprose Iapetus, and Creus too,
And Phorcus, sea-born, and together strode   385
To where he towered on his eminence.
There those four shouted forth old Saturn's name;
Hyperion from the peak loud answered, "Saturn!
Saturn sat near the Mother of the Gods,
In whose face was no joy, though all the Gods   390
Gave from their hollow throats the name of "Saturn!"

Hyperion
BOOK III

THUS in alternate uproar and sad peace,
Amazed were those Titans utterly.
O leave them, Muse! O leave them to their woes;
For thou art weak to sing such tumults dire:
A solitary sorrow best befits   5
Thy lips, and antheming a lonely grief.
Leave them, O Muse! for thou anon wilt find
Many a fallen old Divinity
Wandering in vain about bewildered shores.
Meantime touch piously the Delphic harp,   10
And not a wind of heaven but will breathe
In aid soft warble from the Dorian flute;
For lo! 'tis for the Father of all verse.
Flush every thing that hath a vermeil hue,
Let the rose glow intense and warm the air,   15
And let the clouds of even and of morn
Float in voluptuous fleeces o'er the hills;
Let the red wine within the goblet boil,
Cold as a bubbling well; let faint-lipp'd shells,
On sands, or in great deeps, vermilion turn   20
Through all their labyrinths; and let the maid
Blush keenly, as with some warm kiss surpris'd.
Chief isle of the embowered Cyclades,
Rejoice, O Delos, with thine olives green,
And poplars, and lawn-shading palms, and beech,   25
In which the Zephyr breathes the loudest song,
And hazels thick, dark-stemm'd beneath the shade:
Apollo is once more the golden theme!

Where was he, when the Giant of the Sun
Stood bright, amid the sorrow of his peers?   30
Together had he left his mother fair
And his twin-sister sleeping in their bower,
And in the morning twilight wandered forth
Beside the osiers of a rivulet,
Full ankle-deep in lilies of the vale.   35
The nightingale had ceas'd, and a few stars
Were lingering in the heavens, while the thrush
Began calm-throated. Throughout all the isle
There was no covert, no retired cave
Unhaunted by the murmurous noise of waves,   40
Though scarcely heard in many a green recess.
He listen'd, and he wept, and his bright tears
Went trickling down the golden bow he held.
Thus with half-shut suffused eyes he stood,
While from beneath some cumbrous boughs hard by   45
With solemn step an awful Goddess came,
And there was purport in her looks for him,
Which he with eager guess began to read
Perplex'd, the while melodiously he said:
"How cam'st thou over the unfooted sea?   50
Or hath that antique mien and robed form
Mov'd in these vales invisible till now?
Sure I have heard those vestments sweeping o'er
The fallen leaves, when I have sat alone
In cool mid-forest. Surely I have traced   55
The rustle of those ample skirts about
These grassy solitudes, and seen the flowers
Lift up their heads, as still the whisper pass'd.
Goddess! I have beheld those eyes before,
And their eternal calm, and all that face,   60
Or I have dream'd."—"Yes," said the supreme shape,
"Thou hast dream'd of me; and awaking up

Didst find a lyre all golden by thy side,
Whose strings touch'd by thy fingers, all the vast
Unwearied ear of the whole universe   65
Listen'd in pain and pleasure at the birth
Of such new tuneful wonder. Is't not strange
That thou shouldst weep, so gifted? Tell me, youth,
What sorrow thou canst feel; for I am sad
When thou dost shed a tear: explain thy griefs   70
To one who in this lonely isle hath been
The watcher of thy sleep and hours of life,
From the young day when first thy infant hand
Pluck'd witless the weak flowers, till thine arm
Could bend that bow heroic to all times.   75
Show thy heart's secret to an ancient Power
Who hath forsaken old and sacred thrones
For prophecies of thee, and for the sake
Of loveliness new born."—Apollo then,
With sudden scrutiny and gloomless eyes,   80
Thus answer'd, while his white melodious throat
Throbb'd with the syllables.—"Mnemosyne!
Thy name is on my tongue, I know not how;
Why should I tell thee what thou so well seest?
Why should I strive to show what from thy lips   85
Would come no mystery? For me, dark, dark,
And painful vile oblivion seals my eyes:
I strive to search wherefore I am so sad,
Until a melancholy numbs my limbs;
And then upon the grass I sit, and moan,   90
Like one who once had wings.—O why should I
Feel curs'd and thwarted, when the liegeless air
Yields to my step aspirant? why should I
Spurn the green turf as hateful to my feet?
Goddess benign, point forth some unknown thing: 95
Are there not other regions than this isle?

242

What are the stars? There is the sun, the sun!
And the most patient brilliance of the moon!
And stars by thousands! Point me out the way
To any one particular beauteous star,   100
And I will flit into it with my lyre,
And make its silvery splendour pant with bliss.
I have heard the cloudy thunder: Where is power?
Whose hand, whose essence, what divinity
Makes this alarum in the elements,   105
While I here idle listen on the shores
In fearless yet in aching ignorance?
O tell me, lonely Goddess, by thy harp,
That waileth every morn and eventide,
Tell me why thus I rave, about these groves!   110
Mute thou remainest—Mute! yet I can read
A wondrous lesson in thy silent face:
Knowledge enormous makes a God of me.
Names, deeds, gray legends, dire events, rebellions,
Majesties, sovran voices, agonies,   115
Creations and destroyings, all at once
Pour into the wide hollows of my brain,
And deify me, as if some blithe wine
Or bright elixir peerless I had drunk,
And so become immortal."—Thus the God,   120
While his enkindled eyes, with level glance
Beneath his white soft temples, stedfast kept
Trembling with light upon Mnemosyne.
Soon wild commotions shook him, and made flush
All the immortal fairness of his limbs;   125
Most like the struggle at the gate of death;
Or liker still to one who should take leave
Of pale immortal death, and with a pang
As hot as death's is chill, with fierce convulse
Die into life: so young Apollo anguish'd;   130

His very hair, his golden tresses famed
Kept undulation round his eager neck.
During the pain Mnemosyne upheld
Her arms as one who prophesied.—At length
Apollo shriek'd;—and lo! from all his limbs   135
Celestial   *   *   *   *
             *   *   *   *   *

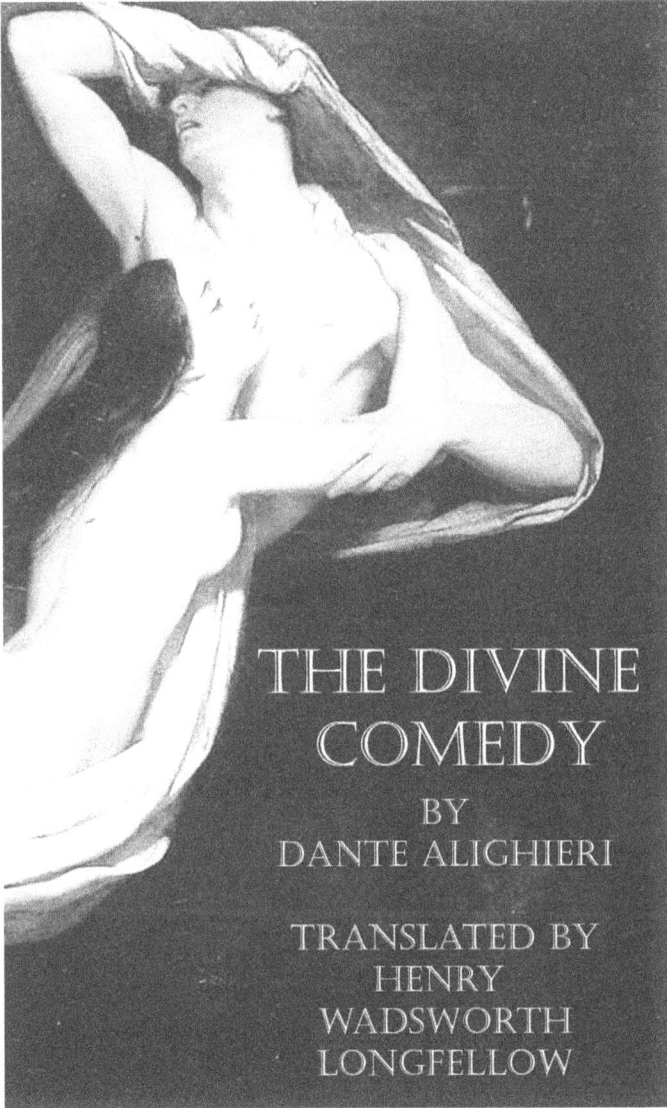

Benediction Classics, Hardback, 2011, ISBN: 978-1849024297

A classic English translation - archaic in tone but never obscure - of Dante's famous poem by the pre-eminent poet of nineteenth century America, Henry Wadsworth Longfellow.

www.ingramcontent.com/pod-product-compliance
Lightning Source LLC
Chambersburg PA
CBHW030522100426
42813CB00001B/115